Soul Travelers
of the Far Country

This book has been authored by and published under the supervision of the Living ECK Master, Sri Harold Klemp. It is the Word of ECK.

Soul Travelers of the Far Country

Harold Klemp

**Illuminated Way
Publishing Inc.**
PO Box 28130
Crystal, MN 55428

Soul Travelers of the Far Country

Printed in U.S.A.
ISBN: 0-88155-056-6

Cover design by Lois Stanfield
Illustrations by Kevin and Scott McMahon and Stan Burgess

To ECK Master Peddar Zaskq
and the
Adepts of the Vairagi Order

Contents

My first contact with the ECK teachings came from
Paul Twitchell, whose spiritual name is Peddar Zaskq.

1

Barriers to God

My first contact with the ECK teachings came from Paul Twitchell, whose spiritual name is Peddar Zaskq. He was the Mahanta, the Living ECK Master when I was stationed at an Air Force base near Tokyo. His ad in *Fate* magazine spoke of Soul Travel, and eagerly I sent for information. At the time, this event seemed of minor importance. Little did I know how it would change my life.

Several weeks later the first ECK brochure came in the mail. The idea of Soul Travel left me spellbound, but I could not guess that the brochure in my hand represented only the smallest fraction of the spiritual instruction to come. The greater part would issue from the inner planes, where Paul would meet and teach me in the Soul body because he had the power to do it. How many religious leaders can say that?

Early in my instruction, Paul addressed a fear put in me long ago by religion—the fear of hell for sins unknown, a barrier too great for one to overcome alone on his ascent to God. Paul began to make me face this fear and so weaken its hold.

By the time I was fourteen, Paul and the other ECK Masters had already begun to manage my spiritual affairs by making arrangements for my first-rate education in a

1

Lutheran school. The teachers there taught about original sin, and that Jesus was the only savior from it. Uncertainty about the biblical teachings nagged at me for years and finally trailed me even to Japan. My questions about life went beyond the concepts of original sin and salvation. I wondered about many things not explained in the Bible: (1) Was creation according to the book of Genesis or evolution? (2) Where did Cain's wife come from in a new world of only three inhabitants? (3) Did Elijah, the prophet, reincarnate as John the Baptist? (4) If Christ was the only crucified savior, what about Krishna of India, Mithra of Persia, or Quetzalcoatl of Mexico—all of whom supposedly died by crucifixion for the spiritual welfare of their followers? (5) Would the Dead Sea Scrolls ever make any kind of significant change in biblical translations and, thus, in the understanding of truth?

To help me resolve these issues Paul made a number of visits to my air base in Japan, in the Soul body. He had me look at a problem from several different angles, to develop confidence in my own judgment as a spiritual being. Mainly, I learned it was OK to ask questions about the Bible.

A year before these meetings with Paul all sorts of harassment had hit me. These were barriers to God sent by the negative power, Kal Niranjan, to create doubt and disturbances. It is, after all, his job to strengthen us through hardship. He is a pest, starting trouble wherever he can, so that a seeker exhausts himself trying to quench the flames that threaten to consume his peace of mind. The Kal, known outside of ECK as Satan, thus scatters our attention to get it off God.

After an individual has spent all his energy to regain control of a life gone sour, he begins to look for spiritual liberation. Then the Master can enter his life.

The play of Satan is therefore not evil for its own sake, but is God's way to fortify Soul. God gave Satan the job of conditioning us by trial. A swimmer who swims every day develops a lean and supple body. His struggle against the resistance of the water builds endurance. In the same way, the Spiritual Exercises of ECK are our way to build spiritual endurance and frustrate the wiles of this negative power, which wants to catch us in its karmic traps.

Freedom is for the strong. Raw courage must exist to safeguard hard-won freedom—be it personal, political, or spiritual. I learned this a year before reading Paul's ad in *Fate* magazine. But when the lesson came it was masked, appearing to have no connection at all with my search for truth.

I learned this lesson about fighting for personal freedom through a fellow airman named Red. Red made me see that struggle may be the only way to get rid of fear.

Red lived down the hall in my barracks, and he had a bad habit of getting drunk and beating people who got in his way. He was a ditty-bopper, a nickname for an airman whose specialty in the service was Morse code; the name derived from the dits and dahs that compose Morse.

The dits and dahs came over Red's radio and ran along a patch cord to his earphones, and from there, up to his brain. Always the dits and dahs were pecking at his brain, and in time they seemed to perforate it. Red's eyes had the gleam of a madman. Already nearly mindless, he forgot and drank to forget some more. Then he beat people up because it felt good. When he and his buddies stormed into town, other airmen fled back to base. Red was a terror, and now word was out that I was his next target.

Why me? Simply because I was in a small group of language specialists, and therefore different. My group was smaller than the Morse group, a minority—a natural target for prejudice. And worse, I was the only language man in this barracks.

3

My roommate was Bob, a ditty-bopper too, but a rung above his friends on the ladder of evolution. We got along well, but it was Bob who brought me the news of Red's plans.

"Red says you're short," he said, with a yawn.

"Short?"

"You're a short-timer."

The term made no sense, so I sat down to think about it. The only definition of "short-timer" that I knew of was a GI who was at the end of his tour of duty. A short-timer was ready to ship out for the States, and he was the envy of everyone, especially those airmen whose orders for home were still months away. But the real meaning of short-timer, as Bob explained, was this: "Red's going to mash your face and beat you to a pulp—that's short-timer!"

Overloaded, my mind went numb.

This was a security base. There was enough tension at work without the added worry of a beating in the barracks. My job could mean the difference between life and death for an American pilot, and I needed rest in order to be fresh for duty. But Red's threats destroyed the refuge of my room.

Red and his friends began to harass me in earnest, hoping I would lash out in anger, and give Red a reason to swing into action. One day a loaf of bread was shredded over my bed, stereo, and desk. Another time, somebody woke me by banging on the door, then laughing wildly as he fled down the hall.

My prayers for help only made things worse, for now the ditty-boppers jostled me in the hall. "Wait'll Red gets you," they bellowed with laughter.

What would happen if he got me?

One day before the afternoon shift, I weighed the situation. No doubt he would win a fistfight, because he had beaten airmen tougher than me. After one beating, what would stop him from doing it again? Could I live with myself, sneaking around the base like a whipped dog in order

4

to avoid the next round?

Just then Bob roared into the room half-drunk, ready to change clothes and report for duty. He stood tottering on one leg, trying to pull the pants leg of his green fatigues over his shoe. After this hopping dance, he finally succeeded in pulling on his pants. He then grabbed a loaf of bread from the table by the window, ripped open the cellophane with his two great paws, scooped out a handful of bread, and stuffed it into his mouth, dry.

"Red's still talking," he mumbled contentedly between chews. The ditty-boppers enjoyed the terror they imagined I must feel.

While Bob stuffed his face like a chipmunk, I was half-listening to a country record, wondering how to save my skin. The answer came out of the blue: "Get the baseballs in your closet." My three baseballs. Red might mangle me in a fight, but I knew how hard I could throw a baseball.

Bob wiped crumbs from his mouth with a hairy forearm, ready to lurch out the door for work. "Give Red a message for me," I said. Bob arched his eyebrows. Deep furrows formed on his forehead as he struggled to push away the curtain of drunkenness.

"Tell him, if I ever get off the floor when he's done with me," I said, "I'm bouncing three baseballs off his head. And I throw hard. Tell him." Bob shrugged, unwilling to get into a cross fire by delivering such a message. But finally resolving something in his mind, he ambled toward the operations building, whistling.

These black storm clouds of conflict passed away quietly, and Red soon shipped out for the States. The ECK had intervened, and his departure was anticlimactic. But the encounter had taught me a little about the need to face fear with courage.

Inner strength comes when there is no place left to turn. Although resigned to a beating, I had no plans for being a full-time doormat. My inner resolve to fight back was a danger signal that warned Red, "Don't tread on me."

5

After this moment of truth had passed, I began to see that many bad situations need not end in violence. One can mock up energy to divert the danger. Paul Twitchell covers these techniques in *The Flute of God.*

Years after this incident, after watching Paul and other ECK Masters develop the spiritual strength of their followers, I learned that a real Master lets no one lean on him for long. Courage is the raw stuff Soul must have if It would see God. To be fully in ECK, a chela puts complete faith in It. He is then beyond fear, and all life reaches out to him.

President Franklin D. Roosevelt once said, "The only thing we have to fear—is fear itself." But better is the inscription on the mantel of Hinds' Head Hotel in England: "Fear knocked at the door. Faith answered. No one was there."

After Red had shipped out for the States, my luck turned around: sudden orders transferred me away from the inhospitable, cold winter of Misawa Air Base, which was on the northern end of the island of Honshu. My new home was down south near Tokyo, at Yokota Air Base; winter was mild there.

It was at Yokota that I first ordered the ECK discourses from Paul, and my spiritual bond with him grew because the spiritual exercises in them made it possible for us to meet each other in the Soul bodies. My early Soul Travel journeys were kept close to home, to a zone near the Physical Plane. He was like the flight instructor who makes sure his student does not fly beyond the immediate vicinity of the airfield and get lost.

All that Soul Travel is, is the skill of shifting into a higher state of consciousness. This often gives one the sensation of traveling swiftly through a comfortable blackness. When the Soul Travel movement stops, the Master tells the chela (student), ''Open your eyes. We're here.''

It was a delightful thing to have Paul appear to me in the Soul body on the inner planes. He made it a point to poke fun at arrogant religious leaders who let their followers make them into frozen god-images. It was a warning for me not to make a living idol of him. Yet I knew, without question, that Paul was indeed the Mahanta, the Living ECK Master.

What did Paul look like during these Soul Travel meetings? Usually he wore a sky-blue shirt with a single pocket on the left side, and his collar button was nearly always open. His slacks were a deep shade of royal blue. His face, although sharply defined in the ink drawing in *Fate* magazine, was rounder and kinder in person. The zest of glowing health was behind his robust tan. He combed his honey-brown hair in a modest wave to the right side. A startling feature was his piercing robin's-egg blue eyes that seemed to penetrate to the very heart of Soul.

One evening in 1967, I crawled into my bunk to do the spiritual exercises from the monthly Soul Travel discourse. A humming sound began in and around my head; it grew inside me, and yet filled the whole room. In time I was to learn that this was one of the many sounds of ECK, the Holy Spirit. The humming tone lifted me upward; then, in full awareness, I—as Soul—slipped from the body as easily as one would squeeze a banana from its peel.

This particular Soul Travel experience began as a dream. Our destination was a sub-Astral Plane, a parallel world to earth that is just beyond its physical boundaries.

The humming sound had taken me out of the body in full awareness. Then I entered into a dream of home; the sound drew me to the lawn outside our farmhouse. To the north of the barn, a gigantic orange planet hung in the sky over the woods. It seemed so close I thought my outstretched hand could touch it. Below it, off to the side, a smaller planet was also in orbit around the earth. This smaller planet was brownish-grey, but orange light reflected on it from the larger one. The color of the orange planet was so pure that I caught my breath in wonder. Suddenly Paul appeared beside me and said, "They are of the Sun and Moon worlds!" In this experience, a dream had turned into the full consciousness of Soul Travel.

Soon after this, Paul began to wean me from the incomplete, and sometimes misleading, religious teachings of my youth. He expected me to sort truth from fiction, to see whether old beliefs held their structure under the microscope of spiritual inquiry. Thus he introduced me to the secret doctrines of ECK.

Through the secret doctrines of ECK, a student of ECKANKAR can be rid of the yoke of karma that makes him a prisoner of himself; his desires will quit him in a natural way, through detachment. Philosophy and symbology merit little, for they are of no value without the Sound and Light of ECK, the only enduring things of God. When he finally receives the Crown of Life, the reward for all his past endeavors is self-determination of the highest order. This is God-Realization.

In my early days as a student of ECKANKAR, I often visited the Temples of Golden Wisdom, including the one on Venus. This temple is called the House of Moksha, which means "house of liberation." It is invisible to human eyes because its vibrations are at the peak of the spectrum of physical matter. The ECK Master in charge there is Rami Nuri, who is aided by other ECK Masters in teaching the Shariyat-Ki-Sugmad, the ECK holy book.

Paul also took me to other Temples of Golden Wisdom, such as the temple of Askleposis in the city of Sahasra-dal-Kanwal, on the Astral Plane; the Sakapori wisdom temple in the city of Honu, on the Causal Plane; the Namayatan temple in Mer Kailash, on the Mental Plane; and the temple of Dayaka in the city of Arhirit, on the Etheric Plane.

These are some of the main temples; there are also hundreds of branch temples of all sizes on every plane of God.

Of interest in the Mental Plane is one unusual country with rich blue soil, just as earth has yellow sand or red clay. The blue soil is used in road construction, and so the highways there are a striking blue.

Such nighttime Soul journeys from Japan to places like this took more time going than coming. Going to these far places was like riding a comet to the stars, but the return was quicker than the snap of a finger. One minute I would be in a temple, lost in thought over some statement by Paul, and then my body would be stirring in bed, in Japan.

Travelers sometimes paint a picture of Askleposis as a grand English cathedral. The public entrance in front is up broad steps, but Paul usually brought me in through a side door. He would lead the way down spacious corridors that ran through the whole building. In one part of the temple, classrooms lined the hallways; rooms for lodging were in another area.

Paul gave three lectures on each visit here. The twelve chelas in one particular class were seated on cushions, in a semicircle. They had come here in the dream state. The youngest was a Chinese boy of twelve. There was also a middle-aged woman with chestnut hair that fell to her shoulders, a jolly gentleman of about forty, and a gaunt and pale man with keen hazel eyes. The whole group seemed to be salt-of-the-earth people.

From my cushion I could see the green leaves of a tree just outside the window. Behind that, the azure sky. This hall of wisdom on the Astral Plane looked similar to buildings on earth, only it was immense beyond description.

Paul stood alongside the dais and rested his foot on it. Leaning forward to face the class, he said, ''The history of mankind is contained in the sacred books of the Shariyat-Ki-Sugmad, whose volumes are kept in halls of wisdom on many planes. Sometimes the words are set on paper, but they often appear in a hologram. The words of the Shariyat may also be transmitted to an individual by the Light of God, in a blinding sheet or on a golden scroll.

"In the beginning, SUGMAD dreamed in the Ocean of Love and Mercy and created Soul from ITS own substance. But Soul began to frolic in the royal gardens of God without regard for the joy of giving. Its selfish nature was of no use in caring for creation, so the SUGMAD dreamed again. This time the Divine Dreamer made a creation of coarse universes below the spiritual planes, where nothing would exist except by interaction.

"The SUGMAD's displeasure opened the windows of heaven, and Soul was dropped into these worlds of dark misery to learn perfect love through the sensations of sorrow and pain. One commandment did SUGMAD give Soul: 'Love me and keep my ways!' The round of births and deaths were to endure until all of Soul's imperfections were gone. Only then could It return to heaven as a Co-worker with God."

As Paul spoke, the ECK Current swept through me in waves, for the Divine Voice was speaking directly to Soul. This made me light-headed, and before long, my mind drifted off down memory lane and I missed much of Paul's lecture.

The flashback took me back to my parochial school. It showed my teacher, a tall and wiry individual in his late thirties, who was quick to discipline children. He led us in daily Bible reading, and every few years we finished the whole Bible, from Genesis to Revelation, by reading a chapter or two a day. Then when it was completed, without a day lost in between, he would start all over again at Genesis.

We read the words, but the quaint language of the King James Bible left us in the dark. Bible reading was mostly an exercise in speed-reading, not a study of deep theology. The idea was to get through our turn as quickly as possible. Still, we were not completely insensitive to the Bible passages we read. Some things did strike us as odd. For

10

instance, my cousin Janice, a fifth grader, raised her hand to ask our teacher the meaning of *bosom*. His face turned the color of ash.

"Why do you want to know that?" he exploded. "Ask your mother." She was crushed by his crude manner, which ended the conversation. He thought she was trying to embarrass him. One could speak of a man's chest, but a woman's bosom?

Our teacher put a damper on touchy questions; I hoped Paul was not like him.

Paul had covered a lot of ground since my thoughts had wandered off.

"A region of deep darkness guards the Soul Plane," he continued. Those with the pure Light of God can cross it, but only with the Light, for this coal black wasteland swallows and loses all but the most spirited. Now and then a daring explorer might find this place on his own, but it is unlikely, because the negative power has a network of deceit in place to garble knowledge about the Soul Plane. The Mental Plane, he is told, is the apex of heaven and nothing lies beyond it. But this is not so. No matter how far one travels into the Far Country, he finds there is always one more heaven to explore.

"The Mahanta, the Living ECK Master wants to make the ECK works available to the human community," Paul continued. "But his usual return for this offering of love is mockery and disbelief. The story of my journey to God in *The Tiger's Fang* is thought of as fiction by many. But each individual has his own reality."

What an opportunity, I thought. Paul, the great Soul Traveler, right here with us. Arms folded across his chest, Paul leaned against the window sill and said to me, as if

11

reading my mind, "Certain things bother you about the Bible. Let me say this: the Bible is a scripture of inspiration more than of fact. It is a latecomer to history, beginning its account of history at the close of the Bronze Age." He fell silent, appearing to want a response.

What could I ask that would be worthy of his knowledge? I groped for deep, significant issues, but all that came to mind was a question about Jesus.

"Was Jesus really God?" I asked.

"Godlike, but not God," he replied. "Every Soul traces Its origin to God, the Creator. The difference between people is simply the degree to which they realize the God state within themselves."

"Who were the sons of God who came unto the daughters of men after the time of Noah?" I said.

"They were of the Seres race, a civilization of giants from the Astral Plane that sent explorers to many planets of our solar system, including earth. Colonizers of planets, they founded settlements practically everywhere. They were ancestors of the Lemurian and Atlantean races who grew to a remarkable eleven feet in height."

My religion teachers had said that Jesus was the only begotten son of God, yet the Bible stated that these ancient men, who had fathered children among the daughters of men, were also "the sons of God." Their offspring became the legendary mighty men of renown, whose memory is dimly recalled in biblical accounts.

Maybe Jesus had been a son of God, but how many other "sons of God" had there been in the past, or even exist today? The ECK is the Spirit of God. St. Paul the Apostle wrote to the Romans (Romans 8:14) that those who "are led by the Spirit of God, they are the sons of God." Can I be a son of God, too? I wondered.

* * *

12

This short exchange with the ECK Master raised a cloud of questions. My study of creation and early man had been stopped by certain knotty issues. Adam and Eve started with two sons, Cain and Abel. Cain killed his brother and now the family was three. He was a fugitive and a vagabond after slaying Abel, afraid of people who might kill him. What people? None, unless his father and mother.

Cain then fled to the east of Eden, to the land of Nod. Now a wife appears on the scene for Cain. Where did she come from? Was she his sister or someone from an old Seres colony?

When she bore him a son, Cain built a city and named it after the child, Enoch. A city for a family of three? Does that make sense? Not unless other people were already in the land of Nod, perhaps a tribe from an original colony of the Seres race.

Plenty of questions, if one dared to ask them.

Paul seemed to anticipate my thoughts; he got right to the point. "Other tribes already existed by the time of Cain and Abel," he said. "Cain's wife was from a rival tribe; all the tribes near Eden were descendants of Atlantis.

"By the time Biblical writers began to gather and transcribe the old word-of-mouth legends, history had long forgotten the sinking of Lemuria and Atlantis. Survivors of these catastrophes made homes throughout the world, including those who settled much later in Eden and Nod. The simple creation story in Genesis was for the simple tribal people of three thousand years ago, and was updated for the early Christians centuries later.

"Reincarnation was known to the Essenes, to Jesus, and to his disciples. It was taught by Zadok, who was the Living ECK Master at the time of Christ. When Jesus told his disciples that Elijah, the Old Testament prophet, had

13

already come, they knew he meant that Elijah had come back as as John the Baptist. This was the old idea of reincarnation.

"The story of Christ's crucifixion for the sake of his followers is borrowed from legends of the Hindus, the Persians, the Greeks, the Celtic Druids, the Mexicans, and others. Krishna, Mithra, Prometheus, Hesus, and Quetzalcoatl were all ancient saints who died by crucifixion. Christianity did not originate the concept of a crucified savior.

"It is doubtful whether the discovery of recent manuscripts, such as the Dead Sea Scrolls, will cause any real change in the doctrines of the traditional church. The old doctrines are binders in the foundation of the church and cannot be snatched from the people, else the church would fall in upon itself."

Paul left his station by the window and said, "Let's conclude this for now." And I awoke back in Japan.

Most of the education on the Astral Plane can be had nowhere else. Rebazar Tarzs, the Tibetan ECK Master, is also a teacher at Askleposis. One time he taught me how to detect the presence of the Angel of Death.

Rebazar is certainly a striking figure. He stands nearly six feet tall and wears a thick, short beard. His hair is coal black, like his eyes. He looks directly at you with a gaze that misses nothing. The robe he wears in the temple is maroon, but in public he dons clothing that is customary to the people of the locality. He does this in order not to excite the attention of any low sorts who might wish to harm him over a small thing like unfamiliar attire.

The ECK Master took me aside to a garden near the temple and said, "The Angel of Death is really an underling in the spiritual order whose duty it is to take uninitiated Souls to the Astral Plane at the time of death. The deceased goes

14

immediately to the Dharam Raya, the judge who reviews the merits of his past life and passes sentence on it. When the account is settled to everyone's satisfaction, the individual is led to his new home. At the reunion with old friends and family members, he is greeted with joy and open arms.

"Years may pass in study and rest before this Soul again feels the familiar tug to return to earth in a new body. This starts another round of experiences in which he will eventually earn the good karma that will let him meet the Mahanta, the Living ECK Master. Only then can he break the chain of reincarnation and find spiritual freedom."

Then Rebazar whispered to me the secret of detecting this angel's presence, but warned, "You've earned this knowledge. It is to help you reach detachment. The secret is for you alone. Understand?

"A person who has not reached the Second Initiation in ECK goes directly to the chambers of the judge of karma when he dies," Rebazar added. "This official of karma is like a customs officer who determines the value of a traveler's purchases. Karma is a use tax that must be paid without complaint or bargaining. The sentence is just in all cases, and the individual accepts it without argument. Everything in the worlds of causality is run according to this system that is regulated by appointed governors.

"A Second Initiate, however, bypasses the lord of karma at death. The Mahanta, the Living ECK Master accompanies him past the courtyard where the uninitiated await their turn before the judge. The Mahanta ushers his disciple by the shortest route to the place prepared for him."

Rebazar left me alone in the garden to contemplate his words. At first it upset me terribly to carry a foreknowledge of someone's translation (death), but the spiritual travelers remind us that death cannot imprison anyone who is in a high state of ECK. Soul is eternal, without beginning or end.

15

The lesson in Rebazar's instruction about the Angel of Death was detachment. Even though I might know of someone's approaching death, I was not to boast of my knowledge.

How strong must be our urge to reach God? Very strong. But at first we don't care much about lofty spiritual goals because they are immaterial to us. So the ECK Masters lead us slowly toward the higher visions. After all, how many of us want spiritual freedom so much that we will fix our full attention upon God in every waking moment? Not many. Accordingly, we start at the lower end of awareness and move into the full consciousness of God a little at a time.

My motivation was immature when I started in ECK. It was all towards learning how to Soul Travel. Nothing about love, wisdom, understanding, Self- or God-Realization. Soul Travel was like a fantastic travel agency, a genie, that fulfilled my wish to leave Japan at will, to travel home to the States, and not be AWOL. But Paul took my spiritual immaturity into account and began to stretch me in all directions. He wanted me strong, able to stand up for what was spiritually right. And he started the lessons of ECK right there in my barracks room; heaven could wait. Often he taught me through encounters with others.

Right after I sent a letter to Paul asking for more information on ECKANKAR, my squadron assigned a roommate to me, Ron. Since my transfer to Yokota, I had enjoyed the good fortune of a room to myself, and I would now certainly miss the privacy.

Ron was a conceited pessimist—a peculiar crosscurrent of emotions—and our time together was a battle of wills. From the first, he was curious about my ECKANKAR mail from Paul in Las Vegas. But Ron's mother must have forgotten to teach him to keep his fingers off other people's mail without permission; it is like stealing. Once I returned unexpectedly to the room to find him scanning one of Paul's discourses to me. Caught in the act, he flung the letter onto my desk. With biting sarcasm, and to switch attention from himself, he asked, "What good is Soul Travel anyway?" To him it lacked substance, perhaps because he had none. But Paul's writings carried the high vibrations of the living power of ECK. Misfortune strikes any who take a stand against It; and Ron certainly had.

He was secretly smoking marijuana, a habit that clashes entirely with the Holy ECK. The drug is spiritually fatal. When a drug user approaches the works of ECK, even by accident, a raging storm will sooner or later tear him to ribbons. It is a primeval conflict between the ECK and Kal, and the individual who won't let go of his narcotic habits will lose everything in life worth having.

As the weeks passed, Ron's personality became even more lopsided than it had been before. He took every opportunity to make fun of Paul and ECK, not mindful of what bitter return such thoughts would have for him. Already haughty, he now began to boss other airmen around. A few of these confrontations ended in scuffles. The few friends he did have camped out in our room for bull sessions that ran beyond regular bedtime hours, lasting until two or three in the morning. I often went without rest.

This conflict eventually came to a head. In our room were two electrical outlets, one for each of us. When I returned from the airmen's club one afternoon, Ron had taken my outlet for himself.

"What are you doing?" I said.

Wild with rage, he grabbed me by my shirt collar and pushed me backward into the bottom of my closet. Dazed, I thought, My clothes look funny from down here. As I lay there I wondered, Why had he pushed me?

Slowly I crawled from the closet. Ron doubled his fists as I stood up and moved toward him, but immediately he backed into a corner and stood there, walled in by a dresser and a desk. The second-floor window was at his back.

"Why'd you do that?" I asked.

"I hit you once, and I'll do it again!" he screamed.

Hit? He pushed me. Anyway, petty issues aside, he was in no position to make threats, because I blocked the only way out from his corner, my body turned sideways in the narrow opening.

"Don't try it," I said in a flat voice. Not a threat, just a promise. My intention was to loft him out the window and into the dense row of shrubs a story below. But he soon realized that his attack was going nowhere; the fight was over when he dropped his fists, and I let him out of the corner. He had gotten the picture: He was about to join the flight crew, but without the advantage of wings. That thought had quickly cleared his head of whatever smoke was in it.

Soon after this Ron shipped out for the Philippines, and the room was mine again. News about him came back through the grapevine: The military police had caught him with drugs. His attacks against other airmen were raised in the case, and Ron's commander pulled a stripe and demoted him. Less rank, less pay.

This story shows the cleansing power of ECK. Spirit and drugs do not mix.

I grew to love Paul beyond words, but he made sure I kept up my inner disciplines. After all, this was not a popularity contest; he was helping me reach ECK Mastership. Other ECK initiates found him to be a warm and chummy Inner and Outer Master, but he kept me stepping along. He was the Mahanta, the Living ECK Master who gave the careful coaching I needed to reach spiritual freedom. He meant to teach me, and anybody else who cared, the

18

wonderful way of ECK.

An entire network of spiritual government carries out the duties of ECK. Near the foot of this hierarchy is the angel, an Astral go-between for minor deities who want a message delivered to someone in the human race. An angel knows astral travel, and goes between the Astral and Physical planes, but has no knowledge of Soul Travel. The angel is thus confined to places below the Causal Plane and knows next to nothing of the Mental or Soul regions. Soul Travel is a way to travel in all the planes of the lower worlds. But in due time, the angel will also meet the Mahanta and begin his own climb to the mountain peak of God Consciousness.

The Bible has many stories of angels on missions for the ECK hierarchy. One known to many ECKists with a Christian upbringing is the story of Balaam and his ass.

The Israelites were nearing the end of their forty-year journey in the wilderness after the Egyptian captivity. They pitched their tents in the plains of Moab, east of the Dead Sea, but their great numbers posed a serious threat to Balak, king of the Moabites, who had a good reason to fear. The Israelites had just destroyed the Amorites, his neighbors, in battle.

Balak, a superstitious man, had trust in the power of spells. So he sent for Balaam, a prophet in the area, to put a curse upon the children of Israel. The king sent out a party of princes, with reward in hand, to coax Balaam to help.

The princes brought the king's message, and Balaam saddled his ass to go with them. During the journey an angel with drawn sword blocked the roadway, but he was invisible to all but the ass, which bolted in fright and ran off into a field. The animal's stubbornness in front of the princes infuriated Balaam. Here he was on this grand mission to save the Moabite nation, but he could not even steer his ass.

Balaam rained blows upon the poor beast, then climbed

19

on its back to continue the journey. The road became very narrow as it passed two walls near a vineyard. Again the invisible warrior of death stood in the roadway, this time with the intention of slaying the prophet. Balaam was unaware of his danger and kicked the sides of the little animal, but it would not pass the angel with the sword of death.

Caught helplessly between the angel and Balaam, the ass finally drove itself against the wall, crushing Balaam's foot. The prophet jumped off, thrashed the ass a second time, and soon got underway again.

The third time the angel blocked the road was at a narrow passage where the ass simply could not get by. The terrified animal brayed in terror and fell to its knees, whereupon Balaam beat it viciously. Balaam's Spiritual Eye was then opened, and he saw the awesome warrior angel, who said, ''If the ass had not avoided me, I would have slain you and saved her.''

During the whole trip the Divine Power was trying to tell Balaam not to go on this mission against the Israelites; It had used the angel and the ass as channels. Balaam's Spiritual Eye had opened just in time to save him.

Today the ECK still gives us inner guidance as it did to Balaam. But first we must remove the barriers between ourselves and It via the spiritual exercises, which take us above human vision and give a broad, impartial look at our problems. Then the way to God is easier.

How could I possibly tell others about these meetings with Paul? I was on a security base. The security officers investigated personnel who had out-of-the-ordinary interests and habits, because the top secret projects on base required stable people to run them. So it was better to keep quiet about Paul and Soul Travel.

After my tour of duty in Japan was up, I was transferred

20

to Ft. Meade, Maryland. It was here that I first saw the 1968 release of *In My Soul I Am Free,* the story of Paul Twitchell; it left me walking on air. The spiritual leader of ECKANKAR, my teacher, was suddenly a well-known personality. Not only that, but my first Soul Travel journey from Japan to Wisconsin was included in the book, too. That inner experience, and the many more to follow, taught me a great lesson: I am Soul and God loves me. What more is there?

Paul gave me secret instructions in the Spiritual Exercises of ECK because I loved God. He also came to give solace when the weight of the world threatened to flatten me. After military service I became a printer and later moved to Texas.

In Texas, the company that hired me employed a certain pressman who hated people, but especially me. His complaints wore thin the nerves of other employees, for it was almost impossible to be around him and remain cordial. It was difficult to keep clear of a blowup, which would only have made matters worse for everyone in the shop. This man had no control over his emotions and so poured out an endless, negative stream of complaint upon the rest of us.

Things finally got so bad that I asked Paul in contemplation to do something to resolve this karma. Several days later, the ECK Adept came in a dream. "You have my guidance and protection," he assured me.

But still nothing changed. Within the week, however, Paul paid another visit in the dream state to let me know he would post himself, in the Soul body, as a security guard in the pressroom. A royal blue smock covered his stocky, muscular body. The ECK Master crossed his arms and remained on guard as a shield between the angry pressman and me, even during the morning and afternoon breaks.

A peculiar thing then happened outwardly. The very day

that Paul visited me on the inner planes, the pressman began to divert his rage to another printer. He now refused to even talk with me, which was a great improvement over the past. A few weeks later the company laid off several employees in a belt-tightening move and this pressman was let go, too. Who could know my relief? But the karma between us was over, and this made for one less barrier to God.

Every day the ECK wants to guide us toward a better spiritual outlook, but we usually miss the signals It sends. In fact, we even get annoyed when Its direction runs counter to our own.

A businessman is late for an appointment and speeds his car along busy city streets. A string of traffic signals turns red against him; he fumes. But could this be the ECK using the signals to fit him into a new time frame? Do the traffic lights delay, or do they really mesh him in with the giant, invisible cogwheels of cause and effect?

He had left home late. This automatically placed him in the next time frame. Speeding, so as to overcome a bad start, is just brushing aside responsibility for that mistake. And speeding increases the risk of another mistake; this time, an accident. Whatever upset his normal schedule, he should accept the fact: like it or not, he is in a later cycle. This is what the ECK is telling him, through the chain of red lights. He should relax and fit in.

A rhythmic pattern is behind every action. When one acts in concert with this rhythm, which is the Sound Current, or ECK, he avoids many barriers to God. He is then in agreement with life, and all is well with him spiritually.

* * *

To get around barriers on the road to God, an individual must find the Sound and Light, the most certain way to spiritual freedom. A simple contemplative exercise to help one do that is this: At bedtime, shut your eyes and look at a blank screen in your mind. This screen is located at the Spiritual Eye, which is slightly above and behind the eyebrows. Breathe deeply several times, then sing God or HU softly for twenty minutes. The full technique, "The Easy Way," is listed in the index of Brad Steiger's *In My Soul I Am Free.*

To add variety to your contemplations, look at the letters ECK, which signify the Holy Spirit. Whatever name you choose, sing it daily. This word may be sung aloud—or silently, if you do not want to disturb another. It is often enough to mentally invite the Mahanta, the Living ECK Master to give you a Soul Travel experience during sleep. No harm will come to you, for a Soul Traveler of the Far Country is always there to watch over you.

Before contemplation, think of some person you love, or of some happy event. This feeling of love or goodwill is necessary for travel in the Far Country. Soul Travel is the first step to God.

Picture yourself walking in the sand at the edge of the water. . . .
Overhead, white gulls sail silently on the wind.

2

The Travelers of ECK

The first ECK Master I met on the inner planes was Paul Twitchell, whose spiritual name is Peddar Zaskq. The next most important ECK Traveler I met was the beloved Rebazar Tarzs. Rebazar is a Tibetan who served as the leader of the ECK community many years ago, when Tibet was the spiritual center of the world and the teachings were taught in secret.

Rebazar is about six feet in height, wears a full beard that is as thick as black wool, and neatly trimmed. His hands are big and square, testimony to the rugged outdoor life he enjoys. Someone who meets him during Soul Travel sees a strong, deeply tanned traveler who is master of every possible situation. His knowledge of the Far Country is extraordinary, and he has given his whole life to helping others find the perfection of God.

Another feature of Rebazar worth noting is his eyes. Like two dark pools in a bottomless sea, they seem to see all, know all. They are eyes of compassion and mercy, all-seeing eyes that serve both as a mirror of Soul and a microscope to the universe. To look into them is to become lost in the Sound and Light of God, the ECK. The liquid of God pours from them like a sweet nectar to fill the emptiness of the heart, and I drank deeply when we met in the spiritual worlds.

This is a fair description of Rebazar Tarzs. He and all the other ECK Masters are Co-workers with the Living ECK Master, who during my term as an ECK novice was Paul Twitchell.

The ECK Travelers are coaches, not mediators; does anyone dare come between God and man? They advise people of the best way to God. A football coach gives his players the advantage of his own years of experience as a player, in addition to all he has learned since then, but the players take the bruises on the field. After all, it's their game. A good coach will see to it that they reach the goal line as quickly and easily as possible.

It is hard to talk about the Far Country because of the limits of human expression. The experiences that take place there have their own language, but perhaps the meetings described here with Rebazar Tarzs will show how the ECK Travelers help people with the burdens of their heart.

Two things needed for Soul Travel are will and knowledge, which combine to create favorable conditions for Soul Travel. The Living ECK Master can pass along the spiritual exercises, but only the individual can rally his will to travel in the Soul body.

This is the exercise I used in contemplation at bedtime. I sang the word *HU* to myself on the outgoing breath and held the note until drawing another breath. HU, a most holy name of God, was the ancient Lemurian's song of upliftment. It was their way to reach the ECK, the Holy Spirit. The Druids held that HU was the highest God, and to the Egyptians the name meant the God of Utterance—a corruption of its real meaning, however.

Any number of things may occur in contemplation, but for several weeks I had no experience whatsoever. Yet curiosity drove me on with this spiritual exercise because I sensed a real substance behind the ECK teachings, even though it seemed to take forever to see the proof of experience. But, really, what is a delay of a few days, months, or even years? Novices of other paths to God have spent entire lifetimes in search of a single experience to assure them that they were indeed on the right path.

So here I sat in contemplation, singing HU with eyes lightly shut. To avoid falling asleep, I sat on the floor rather than take a chance of lying down in bed. My back was solidly braced against the bed to forestall tipping over and ruining the session. Thus settled in, I felt ready for the Winds of God, should they come. My mind was free of worry, open to receive any vision from the inner planes.

Our breath is a sound of HU as we breathe in and out. My object was to go out, to Soul Travel, so the natural thing was to sing HU on the outgoing breath. Without straining, I then watched the inner screen of my mind, which was blank to start, in an offhand, easy way.

This was my experience: A single pinpoint of white light appeared in the depths of the dark universe before me. It was far off in the distance but exploded toward me at a fantastic speed, like a brilliant sun racing from the other side of the universe to swallow me in the hotness of its light. Now I flew toward it, like a tiny dot of light racing to meet a planet of unspeakable radiance.

It was like flying into the sun, passing through a curtain of light, and coming out on the other side to a world of gorgeous colors. I hung suspended in space, a splendid light (the glorious Soul body) of seeing, knowing, and being.

Below me lay the dazzling white sands of a beach, with a multiplicity of blue-and-green ocean waters; the waves washed mildly upon the sand. Small birds ebbed and flowed with the tide, mirroring the give-and-take of life. The bright blue sky was unclouded by haze of any kind. This must be heaven, I thought.

In the next instant, I was atop a high cliff overlooking the ocean. How can one describe the perception of Soul, since, despite this great height, it was possible to see and hear as if my feet were walking in the warm sands of the beach below?

"Look, in the distance!" commanded a deep baritone voice beside me.

Startled, I looked around. It was Rebazar Tarzs, the Tibetan ECK Master, who no doubt was my benefactor in providing this trip to a most beautiful heaven of God. Gripped in his powerful right hand was a stout walking staff of shoulder height. With his left, he pointed far down along the beach, where two dark figures were walking.

Suddenly, from our vantage point on the steep cliff, the distance between us and the two specks collapsed. Time and space had both crumbled. My spiritual vision jumped to the two figures in a twinkling and showed a man and a woman slowly walking the beach toward us. To my surprise, the smallish man was my friend and Master, Paul Twitchell—the Mahanta. The other person was a young woman in a flowing white gown that billowed softly around her in the gentle sea breeze. Slender, with brunet hair, she stood somewhat shorter than Paul. Pain and trouble had drawn her face into a tight band, and she plodded beside him as if in a daze.

The two beach walkers passed well below our observation point on the cliff. A cloak of light surrounded us, and Rebazar made the comment, "This warm light that bathes us is from the Ocean of Love and Mercy. It is the Holy Spirit and is a reflection of the light from the atoms of God." Rebazar's ruby red robe was barely to be seen in this mist of golden light, which seemed to enwrap me too, although I could not see myself.

"This sphere of golden light is the Soul body," he said, "the highest of the forms of man."

On the beach below, the heavy-hearted woman trudged beside Paul. A shuffling trail in the sand marked their slow passage, meandering footsteps at the edge of lapping wavelets. Paul saw us on the cliff and waved his hand, but an invisible screen shielded us from the woman. They inched along the beach, slowly shrinking in the distance. A long way off stood a lighthouse, their destination.

"The sorrows of life have cut sharply into the spirit of that young one," Rebazar remarked, compassion modulating his musical voice. His speech was not in outer tones, yet it came through the electric atmosphere of this remote world of God as clear as a bell.

"The body is perishable and must return to dust, as will all corruptible creation," he said. "That Soul has loved God too dearly, for she has not learned to discriminate in giving love. Amid the confusion of agony, she tried to cut the silver cord and break the golden vessel."

Rebazar spoke of the Preacher in Ecclesiastes, who said: "Or ever the silver cord be loosed, or the golden bowl be broken..." The silver cord is the lifeline between the physical body and its higher counterparts; the golden bowl is the aura around the head. The woman had tried to commit suicide, but the Mahanta stepped in to prevent it. For months thereafter, he took her out of the body at night and brought her to this serene paradise by the sea for spiritual healing.

"Her emotional and mental repair will take time," concluded Rebazar. "Come, let us go."

I took a last look at the ocean and the beach, and suddenly understood that the sparkling, celestial waters of this ocean were inexperienced Souls who awaited the right conditions for rebirth into the physical world. Then, in an instant, I was home in my room.

The Masters of the Vairagi Order usually teach those new in ECK through the dream state, rather than by Soul Travel, because most of these newcomers are used to dreams. The Adepts want to assure them of a smooth transition from the human to the higher consciousness. Why jump someone along the spiritual path faster than he is able to go? The ECK Travelers know the delicate nature of the seeker and let him set his own pace on the road to God.

During sleep, the ECK dreamer learns to put his waking concerns into the care of these travelers, who lead him to the Mahanta, the Inner Master. The chela discovers the Light and Sound of God and then knows that the Living Word of God is lost in mankind's ragged scriptures.

St. John called the Light and Sound the Word. Holy men of the East call It the Bani, the teaching of the inner music. The Audible Life Stream, the Sound Current, and the Holy Ghost are all one and the same. They are but different names for the ECK, the Life Force, the common bond between life forms everywhere. The ECK is the force of creation, the power that illumines Soul and brings spiritual freedom.

These travelers of the Vairagi Order came to take me to the Far Country, which the same Preacher in Ecclesiastes called "the long home." Paul Twitchell was my first visitor; he was the Mahanta, the Living ECK Master from 1965 to 1971, and brought ECKANKAR to the public in this age. But there were other ECK Masters, like Rebazar Tarzs, who helped him develop me spiritually though Soul Travel.

One indication of the Mahanta's presence is the Blue Light. It may look like a Japanese lantern, or a blue glow, or speckles of blue starlight. The Blue Light is seen by people under all conditions, even by those doing chores around the home, but especially during contemplation or in the dream state. The Blue Light may appear in moments of serenity and repose, but also during distress, danger, or sickness.

Carl Jung, founder of analytical psychology, saw the Blue Light as a child when he was very ill. Coughing seizures left him in terrible pain, but they eased whenever the Light appeared. But it is doubtful that he ever made the connection between the Blue Light and the Mahanta.

30

The ECK Travelers, such as Rebazar, guard those who are loyal to ECK, or who have earned the right to come to ECK in this lifetime through some merit from the past. They give protection in the most dire circumstances, and their intervention is a princely gift, although few will recognize it.

Rebazar once saved the life of a sailor in World War II, and this is how it happened. It was 1942. A German submarine had sent a torpedo into a commercial vessel eighty miles from New York. The crew took to the lifeboats, and for two weeks the men were adrift in the Atlantic. Their numbers thinned as food and water rations ran out.

One young sailor, who felt his time on earth was over, was surprised to find himself out of the body, suspended above the lifeboat in the Soul body. He could clearly see the pitiable condition of his dying companions, and his own physical body, like a rag, in a heap at the bottom of the boat.

In the Soul body, he was cloaked in a pleasant wave of golden light that stretched to eternity. The most enjoyable part of being out of the body was the warmth he felt, a gratifying change from the freezing cold in the tossing lifeboat.

So this is death! he thought, content to remain in this state of love and grace forever. But his reverie was suddenly shattered.

"Go back!" boomed a deep voice in the space around him. His desire to stay in this blissful state was rebuffed.

"You must return to your body!"

"Never!" shouted the sailor. But he was powerless to defy this powerful being, whom he mistook for God. A spiritual charge that caused no pain electrified the air around him, and then he was back in his body in the bottom of the boat.

Rescuers spotted the boat soon after, and the survivors were given medical attention. But from that day on, the sailor had no fear of death. Unlike the majority of people, he had touched the hem of God's garment, the grace of expanded consciousness. He was never the same man again. The curtains that hide the profound secrets of life and death had parted for him, and the immense wave of golden light he saw was the comfort and warmth of the Holy Spirit; Its voice spoke through the ECK Master Rebazar Tarzs.

The sailor went on to remarkable success in business. Years passed, and upon the death of his wife, he confided this story to his son, an ECK initiate. The father had never spoken of this near-death experience to anyone else, because he feared what people might say.

It is a privilege to be able to learn about Soul, man's real Self. Soul Travel is merely the natural and joyful act of shifting one's consciousness from the Physical body to the Astral, Causal, Mental, or Etheric bodies. It is the act of meeting Soul, the highest Self.

Everyone who goes to sleep is out of the body. A dream is nothing more than one's experience beyond the physical plane, and even those who claim not to dream are really out of the body when asleep. Soul Travel, then, is the conscious movement of Soul between the outer and inner selves, and gives one the ability to remember what the average person does not. Stop and think about it: In sleep, you are naturally out of the body.

The Spiritual Exercises of ECK help us have spiritual experiences in the sleeping hours. Many Higher Initiates have learned the art of being aware during most of a twenty-four-hour day, because they know how to use the periods of normal sleep for unfoldment. While the body sleeps, Soul makes journeys of seeing, knowing, and being. At bedtime, we simply place our thoughts upon some ideal, such as the Sound or Light of God. This image is gently held in mind for about twenty minutes. When sleep comes, an ECK Master is always nearby for protection, should we need it.

Contemplation helps us to sharpen our spiritual ideal.

Daily practice manifests a worthy goal, such as having the Light and Sound in our life, meeting with an absent loved one, or gaining love, wisdom, freedom, or understanding. All of these are uplifting ideals for one's contemplative sessions.

Here is one way to leave the body via Soul Travel. Lie down after dinner when you are drowsy. Plan to nap for five minutes and watch the process of falling asleep. If you try the exercise with your spouse, agree to meet outside the body a few minutes later. Then watch carefully as your mate steps free of the physical body and enters the spiritual one in a burst of radiant light.

One always goes out of the body when he falls asleep, but it is an unconscious act. In Soul Travel, the only difference is that we are trying to get out of the body in full awareness.

The moment Soul leaves the body, It finds Itself in a blue-grey zone near the Physical Plane. This zone is an approach to the Astral Plane. The sensation of moving from the Physical to the Astral body is like slipping through a large iris of mild wind currents; this iris is the Spiritual Eye. Soul enters this neutral zone of blue-grey tones in Its Astral form, a sheath which looks like a thousand sparkling stars.

This buffer zone, or corridor, between the Physical and lower Astral planes, resembles the underground silo of an enormous rocket that is perhaps two hundred feet in diameter and more than two thousand feet deep. The ceiling of this circular pocket is open and may display a brilliant canopy of white light, or you may see a night sky sprinkled with specks of twinkling stars. There may even be a pastoral scene by a river, whose waters murmur their pleasure at life.

Whatever scene is displayed in the opening of that vast ceiling, Soul is drawn toward it at a mighty speed. Most people begin to recall their dreams only after their departure from this launching zone between the two worlds, and after their arrival at a faraway destination on the Astral Plane.

It is true that everyone is not ready for ECKANKAR and Soul Travel. There are few individuals who really want to know who and what they are; the majority of people are afraid to face and master their shortcomings. But that's the key to spiritual strength. Their security is in the hollow contents of their minds, and they shrink from any involvement with Soul.

Soul knows the past, present, and future. But deep knowledge in the hands of the public is a threat to those in power. In *CYCLES: The Mysterious Forces That Trigger Events*, Edward Dewey tells how he once gave a lecture on the natural cycles of business. After his talk, a retired board chairman of one of the largest insurance companies in the country told an associate, "It's all right to play with this cycle business if you are sure there is nothing to it. But if you ever come to believe that this fellow Dewey has something, drop it like a hot potato. There would be nothing worse for the human race than to be able to know the future."

He felt that if the future were common knowledge, it would harm business. This study of cycles, if extended to people's private lives, might mean that an individual would know the very moment to buy health or car insurance. If he could tell by some sort of a chart when to take out a policy against an inevitable accident, the insurance companies would fold.

The Mahanta, the Living ECK Master—and the ECK Masters like Rebazar Tarzs—teach qualified initiates the ECK-Vidya, the ancient science of prophecy. Candidates are put through a grueling selection process because of the high ethics that must accompany this knowledge: Its use is reserved for edifying the human race. In a sense, the fears of religious and political leaders are justified—knowledge in the wrong hands is a danger to society.

A professional jealousy often guards knowledge. We

would like to believe that those with superior knowledge would gladly share it, but a selfish stance such as jealousy may hinder research that would be for the good of all.

A young man was once in school to be an eye doctor. His eyesight became very poor from all the reading, but his optometrist assured him that his vision would stabilize during his early thirties. Instead, his eyesight became worse. The young man began to wonder why a patient always needed stronger lenses each time he saw his optometrist.

When he later had his own practice, he quite by chance stumbled upon research in the field of optics that promised to reduce the need for lenses for a certain group of patients. His interest in this field earned him a right to speak at a national conference on eye care. In his speech, he told of this pioneer work, but when he asked for questions from his audience of eye specialists, he was disturbed that not a single doctor asked for more details about his findings.

An associate explained later that such probing into new technology made his colleagues afraid. What if this research did away with poor eyesight? What would eye doctors do for a living?

Rebazar Tarzs and the other ECK Masters deal with people's confusion and ignorance all the time. But as the ECK Masters help individual Souls reach God Consciousness, a by-product is spiritual upliftment for all. One person's quest for God-Realization will touch many people he has never met, because, as a pathfinder, his discoveries in ECK are a light to the world.

Once, during a short contemplation in my garage room in Pasadena, Texas, I suddenly found myself in the Soul body. Rebazar had brought me to a hilltop near a mountain chain that was rugged like the Alps. We rested from our climb in the ankle-deep pasture covering the hill. Soft white clouds slipped by the range of foothills around us; it was an idyllic spot for reflection.

"All life is from ECK," said Rebazar. "This Word, or Spirit, is in all living things, even in the steadfast rock formation of this hill. The ECK is the Audible Life Stream that descends through all planes unto the far end of creation."

"How did the early ECK Masters replace ignorance with knowledge among the prehistoric tribes of mankind?" I asked. "Today we do the spiritual exercises to survive the grind of daily living. How did the Masters teach ECK to those early people so that their lives would be better?"

"The first concern of primitive man was survival for himself, his family, and the members of his clan," said Rebazar. "When man first left the safety of the treetops to challenge the great beasts for food on the ground, the ECK Masters taught him to make and use weapons. They had already taught him his first language, made up of simple musical sounds that were brought from the Astral Plane. Now our ancestor learned to sing of the hunt, his victories over the enemy, and his yearning for a better life.

"The story of the Tower of Babel is an allegory of how the growth in languages brought confusion to early civilization. As the tribes grew and spread out into more lands, the musical language of one tribe was no longer like that of another. This babbling in tongues caused problems, because no one understood his neighbor. ECK Masters, like Malati, then introduced sign language to combat the linguistic turmoil. Able now to address common needs, the tribes began trade routes to distant neighbors."

It seemed to me that the survival concerns of early man were much simpler than ours today. If the ECK Masters taught him homely truths like tonal and sign language, how significant is a teaching that serves such a limited range of human development? So I asked Rebazar the timeworn question, "What is Truth?" I wondered why anyone would come to ECK when every other religion claims it has the way, the truth, and the life.

"First, ECK is timeless," said Rebazar. "Its message is transformed in every age to fit that consciousness. It was given to primitive man in the only way he could understand: through teaching him the uses of fire, how to make clothes from the skins of animals, and in developing methods for tilling the fields.

"The ECK Masters today give the message in the very terms that people can understand. Many minor teachers also claim to be dispensers of truth, and they draw followers who share their own limited state of consciousness.

"But without the Word, the ECK, who can say he has truth?" asked Rebazar.

"Soul's single purpose in life is to come into harmony with Spirit," he added. "Life's school of hardship buffs smooth the sharp edges of bitterness, anger, passion, miserliness, pettiness, scorn, dishonesty, small-mindedness, perversion, lust, meanness, poverty of Spirit, corruption, vanity—and every other negative trait that comes to mind.

"The passage of Soul through Its incarnations is a search for agreement with ECK, for It is then at one with life. This state is the fulfillment of all love and joy.

"Harmony is love, and love brings joy, understanding, wisdom, goodness, generosity, charity, goodwill—but more than anything else, it brings spiritual freedom. Soul wants to be free. To have freedom, It must become a God-Realized being. Experience in the Sound and Light of God is the most direct way to wisdom, power, and freedom. The way, the truth, and the light is via the Spiritual Exercises of ECK."

Years ago, when I was a Second Initiate, Rebazar Tarzs invited me to a stately Astral city that reminded me of a grander version of London. Rebazar was clean shaven, so

I did not recognize him until he spoke: There is no mistaking his crisp baritone voice once you hear it.

He said that Paul Twitchell was at a training retreat in the city. Did I want to see him? The invitation was more than I'd hoped for; I agreed immediately.

When we arrived in the city of cathedrals, palaces, broad avenues, and spacious parks, Rebazar took me to our lodging and put a call through to Paul, asking for an appointment. Paul granted it and sent back a reply that was both comforting and disconcerting at the same time: "Please don't say I've forgotten you."

In one short sentence he got to the heart of the problem. I had not seen Paul on the inner planes for days and so did indeed feel neglected in my study of ECK, but it bewildered me how he would know. One may study ECK for years, always sure of the Mahanta's presence, even taking it for granted, but then suddenly it is gone. Long stretches of time may pass where the chela, to all appearances, is on his own. Still, the Master is in the background, watching him make his own decisions.

Paul said he would try to work me into his schedule that afternoon at three. Rebazar took me by train to see Paul on the far side of the city. The train was short, only three cars that hovered over a flat track, but it conveyed us briskly to our destination. When we arrived at the station, a short walk brought us to an office building that looked like the consulate of a wealthy country.

By some misfortune I lost track of Rebazar in the crowds that bustled in the halls lined with offices and consular departments. At first this place looked like a government office, but later I realized that it was the main headquarters of the ECK Masters in the city of Sahasra-dal-Kanwal.

I was completely lost. Paul's message on the phone remained in my mind: "Please don't say I've forgotten you." But being lost did little for my self-esteem. What would happen to my spiritual life if I missed this appointment with the Mahanta?

My search for Paul grew frantic, and I pushed open a huge oak door marked "Consul." The room was well lit, but there were no lamps or windows to account for the illumination. Light was everywhere, but nowhere did it cast a shadow. This room appeared to be the bedchamber of a Middle-Eastern sultan. A sleepy guard approached to send me along, but a hand browned by a life outdoors parted the curtain disclosing a canopied bed. On it sat a dignified old man in a cross-legged position.

"Come in, come in," he urged. I hesitated at the door.

"Perhaps you can tell me about religion." His tone suggested that he wouldn't be easily convinced about anything I said, so I declined his invitation.

"I don't know anything about religion," I said.

"Don't be so humble, my son. I have yet to meet anyone without some opinion about religion."

This was actually a test to see whether I had the courage to talk about ECK to someone who asked for truth. Fortunately, the old consul—for that is what he seemed to be—persisted in his request and gave me a second chance to speak of religion.

Boldly I said, "Would you care to hear about another Master, one other than Christ?"

To my surprise, he passed a newspaper article to me about Paul, which called him a "true child of God." Not until later did I know that this snowy-haired gentleman before me was Fubbi Quantz, an ECK Master known to many ECK initiates.

"Yes, I've heard of many fakes," he said, "but this Paul Twitchell is one of the biggest!"

"Ah!" I cried happily. "Then you've heard of Paul? Now, there is truly a Master! He answers the age-old Buddhist prophecy of the new savior who would be born on a body of water, with horses grazing on its banks. He would not sit in the Oriental cross-legged fashion (as you are), but in a chair, feet on the floor, like an Occidental."

At that time I did not realize that this prophecy was

about Paul's previous incarnation, before he came into this one to finish training for spiritual Mastership.

While talking with the elderly consul, I stood with my back turned half toward him, as if torn to stay and teach— as he had invited me to do—or to leave because of the strangeness of this authoritative and grand atmosphere.

"Why are you turned from me?"

"I don't know whether to stay or go."

"Then sit down," he ordered. "We can't have you half in and half out of the room."

A curly, black-haired young boy of five or six had been on a chair beside the bed of the old man when I entered. The child seemed extremely adultlike in demeanor, and the old man now said kindly to him, "Come back later when I call." The boy walked from the room like a miniature king.

"Sit here," the old man said to me. He pointed to the chair vacated by the boy. "Bring your chair closer and let me see your palm."

He began to study the lines in my palm and even the lines on the back of my hands. Then he also examined the shape of my arms and face—to determine my future, he said. His touch was electric and caused a definite tingling sensation.

"You have a great deal of psychic power," I remarked, because I doubted whether his energy was truly spiritual.

"We're going to test your so-called Master, Paul," he said. "Imagine his face, please."

While I closed my eyes and used my imagination to see Paul's face, the old man tuned in to my vibrations. As they rose higher and higher, I was pleased to see Paul's face shine brightly on my mental screen.

From a far-off distance came the old man's voice, as if he were in another room, but I kept my eyes shut. "Yes, he must be all right as a Master, because your vibrations are surely very strong!" he said. My vibrations continued to rise beyond heights I had ever imagined could exist.

There was a knock on the door, and the old man said to

me, "That's all. You may awaken." Rebazar came into the room, a broad smile on his face.

"You kept your appointment with Paul?" he asked.

I nodded, now making the connection between Paul's shining face on my inner screen and the outer appointment I thought I had missed. After that, the old consul invited us to watch an adventure film with a group of other ECK chelas, but long before it ended, Rebazar said, "You are tired. Let's go home."

Awakening in my bed at home, I thanked Paul, who was the Mahanta until September, 1971 when he died, for letting me hang on to the shirttails of ECK one more time.

The spiritual life of one in ECK is in the care of the Mahanta. The Master turns him over to another ECK Master for a particular lesson in the secret knowledge of healing, prophecy, Soul Travel, or of reading the spiritual character of others. Nearly all of these other ECK Masters have been the Mahanta, the Living ECK Master in their day, but now they move quietly in the background of spiritual affairs.

All ground is holy to them; every duty, sacred. Their humility shines like the golden morning sun. They teach that the glory of God is revealed equally in the small things of life as in the large. Public acclaim is nothing to them, only total service to God.

The ECK Masters encourage initiates to be models of action which benefits all. If something is done in this context for love, it is a service to God and is an indication of the spiritual stature of its creator.

An example of this is the story of Abraham Lincoln and his Gettysburg Address. The American nation was torn by civil war. The North had won a great battle over the South at Gettysburg in July 1863. Now, in the same year, a commission was ordered to establish a national cemetery at the site of the battle.

The committee made plans to hold the dedication on November 19 and invited Edward Everett, a popular classical orator, to make the keynote address. Almost by chance, a suggestion was made to invite President Lincoln as a token of respect, but the Pennsylvania commission in charge of the ceremony had doubts that the president could deliver a suitable talk for such a momentous occasion. Nevertheless, the invitation was finally sent.

Lincoln had many weighty matters on his mind. For one, his son Tad was sick in bed. Lincoln's annual report to Congress was also due, and the Civil War always brought details that needed attention. Yet he took a train to Gettysburg, and while on it, he rewrote the first draft of a speech roughed out earlier in his Washington office. And in his hotel room that night, Lincoln finished the final draft of his Gettysburg Address.

At the dedication ceremony the next day, Everett, the eloquent orator, spoke for nearly two hours to the crowd of fifteen thousand people. A song followed his speech, and then Lincoln was presented as the next speaker. His address was short: a bare three minutes.

Lincoln opened with the famous words: ''Four score and seven years ago...'' Then, in simple, classic terms, he stated that the great Civil War was but a continuation of the task of freedom begun by the founders of America. This simple, yet poetic, address stands as a hallmark of freedom's battle against slavery. But when the address was over, he told an aide in private that his speech was a failure.

The next day, however, Everett sent him a letter of congratulations. Everett said he wished that his own central idea, which had taken two hours to deliver, could have expressed so well what Lincoln's did in a few minutes.

Lincoln humbly replied that each of them had a role to play in giving their speeches. The people would not have excused Everett for a short speech, nor Lincoln for a long one. Lincoln's address stands as a masterpiece of modern literature. Yet, from his viewpoint, it was of little consequence. Desperately pressed for time by the concerns of his office and the nation, he nevertheless put his heart into the Gettysburg Address. In so doing, he touched greatness.

The ECK Masters want initiates to strive for spiritual freedom, even as Lincoln fought to achieve freedom for the slaves. But above all else, to take the extra step in being a channel for ECK, because of such are the future Masters of the Vairagi Order.

With these thoughts of Lincoln and freedom in mind, I went into contemplation to reflect upon the element of truth that I dearly wanted to believe underlies all existence—an absolute truth that is always the same, a changeless truth for today, tomorrow, and evermore. That is what I wanted.

A warm chuckle rippled in my garage room. I looked up from my bed to see Rebazar Tarzs behind the counter at the foot of the bed. He sat on a tall stool and leaned his elbows on the countertop.

"You want the riddle of truth?" he asked, his black eyes flashing with merriment. It puzzled me that he should laugh in the same breath as speaking of truth. I was a seeker, a serious seeker of truth. What was funny about that?

"Whoever has even a shred of truth has received it from the ECK Travelers," he continued in a more serious vein. "Truth causes conflict to storm in the heart of man, tearing him every which way. For anyone trained in orthodox religion, it is painful to separate truth from the dogma he has come to revere. But until man stops his search for truth, he cannot have freedom, because truth in an imperfect creation is not whole. This is the riddle of truth.''

This was really confusing. ''How can there be freedom without truth?''

''Only truth from the spiritual worlds of God is pure, but when man is given a single, raw thread of truth to occupy him for a while, he attaches so much importance to it that he won't let go of it later for the finer cloth of the weaver's loom. He wants truth, but not if it means first throwing out the old, ragged thread in hand.

''Try to understand this: Perfect truth is not given to the human state because it cannot comprehend it. The ECK Travelers do reveal higher degrees of truth to us, but eventually, if we are to attain the highest states of God, we must surrender all in our hearts and minds so that selfless love can enter in.

''Truth for a pauper is different than it is for a king, because the experiences of each are so unlike in life; the totality of one's experiences forms his state of consciousness. No two people are alike; therefore, neither is their perception of truth. Whatever the human state claims as knowledge is certainly not absolute truth, and the only way to reach the heights of spirituality is by the ECK, the Sound and Light of God.''

Listening to Rebazar made my head swim. I agreed with what he said, but if anybody had asked me then to recount his words, I would have been at a loss to do so. It would take a great deal of time and thought to put the pieces together in some order.

This reminded me of the philosophy professor who invited me into his office for a discourse on the factors that mislead us into accepting variations of truth for truth itself. After leaving his office, I felt like the recipient of a great treasure. But to retell his dissertation was beyond me, because he spoke of things of which I had no experience.

Rebazar had gone to the window and pushed aside the faded curtains for a look outside. Then he sat down in the orange easy chair next to my bed.

"Thomas Merton, the Roman Catholic mystic, trailed the elusive way to God until he ended up with his face in the dust," he said. "Then Merton realized that God wanted more from him than introspection or devotion. Merton's real goal, and that of all of us, was to go beyond the poverty of the mind and become a Co-worker with God. This means letting go of shopworn truths from the past."

Rebazar leaned back in the orange easy chair, his eyes closed and his arms on the armrests. He was giving me a chance to review what my inner life had been before ECK.

In 1967, after I got into the swing of the spiritual exercises, a definite change took place in my inner worlds. For one thing, I began to remember past lives. It took awhile to grow used to this in-depth spiritual psychology, to see the influences that had made me what I was today. In my case it was true: Since my experiences in ECK, my inner values and my understanding of truth had completely changed.

The ECK Traveler stirred in his chair. "You have seen?" he asked. At my nod, he said, "I must go, but look within your Spiritual Eye, the sacred place above and beyond your eyebrows."

Curious, but obedient, I lay back on the bed and shut my eyes. But when I peered once more at the chair, it was empty. Rebazar had gone as quietly as he had come.

I sang HU while looking directly into my Spiritual Eye and soon was flying through time at an incredible speed. This was actually an illusion because Soul, in Its purity, does not travel. Yet, in the realm of duality, Soul has the perception of time and space as events rush toward It from the place where It has centered the attention.

When the feeling of movement stopped, I was in the familiar golden form of the Soul body. Beside me was Peddar Zaskq—Paul Twitchell, in everyday life. He also wore a golden, radiant body. The scene before us was a country setting. In the near distance were towering mountain peaks that looked like the Rocky Mountains of western America.

"Below us is an animation from the Time Track," said Paul, in his quaint Southern accent. "We are on the Causal Plane, the Third Plane, storehouse of memories and karmic seeds."

A country road cut through a blanket of snow that covered the fields from a recent storm. Cars had left ruts, marring the white apron of ground cover. Our attention was drawn to the distant squeal of brakes that signaled a yellow school bus making a stop at a mailbox a quarter mile away. Two small figures stepped from the bus and bounded toward a house set back several hundred feet from the plowed road. The bus began to creep toward us.

"The year is 1955," said Paul quietly. "The next bus stop is here. Watch!"

In our golden sheaths of light, the Soul bodies, we hung above the landscape, yet seemed a part of it. Everything had an amazing clarity to it: the tracks of rabbits—two hind feet spread apart and accent marks from the two smaller front feet between them; tiny mice trails under the snow; bird dances; brown wisps of grass hiding beside cedar fence posts; the white smoke from the chimney of the home into which the children had gone. I could see it all, but without the unpleasant sting of the winter cold.

The bus plowed through the winding ruts and made its own as the driver shifted gears. Inside the bus, ready to step from the front door, was a young girl who looked like an old acquaintance.

In response to my question about her, Paul said, "It is the woman who walked on the beach with me when you were with Rebazar, only now she is still a child. Remember, the year is 1955."

The brakes squealed in protest as the driver pulled alongside a mailbox near us. The dark-haired girl clutched

46

a cake dish tightly against her thin winter coat, and her lackluster eyes began to sparkle as she pictured herself inside the home where her mother's love would warm her more than any kitchen stove.

"It's February 14," remarked Paul. "Valentine's Day."

The front door of the bus swung open and the girl stepped gingerly down the steps, careful not to fall in the slippery snow. The door snapped shut as the driver, impatient to make up lost time caused by the icy roads, popped the clutch, and the bus lurched forward.

The following sequence happened in a split second. Just before the bus began to roll, the girl, burdened with bulky schoolbooks and the cake dish, peeped cautiously over her load to look at the ground. But a misstep in a car rut threw her under the bus, in front of the dual back wheels. A red flash of alarm struck me as I saw the danger, but how could I pull her to safety with this glowing body of Soul, which was without any more substance than a golden light form?

Then I saw him. Rebazar! He appeared beside the school bus as if by magic. His attire seemed much too scanty for such cold weather: a knee-length red robe with a dark binding to tie the waist. On his feet were sandals, yet the freezing cold had no untoward effect upon him.

Time stood still. Quickly Rebazar grasped the child's free hand and swung her clear of the wheels just as the tires smashed the cake dish into splinters. Dazed, the girl looked up into the kind eyes of her rescuer. The bus lumbered down the country road as the white faces of her classmates pressed against the windows.

Rebazar vanished in that instant. The girl made an effort to brush the wet snow from her coat, frowned at the shattered cake dish, then trudged toward home. She pushed open the front door and stamped the snow from her boots on the hall rug. She called to her mother in the kitchen. "I broke the cake dish, Mom, but I didn't mean to."

A handsome woman with light brown hair emerged from the kitchen. Concern lined her face as she asked for an explanation. When told the story of the near accident, she realized that she had a gift far greater than any cake dish— a live and healthy child.

Paul drew my attention from the house to the subject of cause and effect. "The Causal Plane is the storehouse of karmic seeds" he said. "But one who is destined to find ECK in this life may be spared an 'accident' no longer needed to repay a karmic debt from the past.

"Karma is the effect of a positive or negative deed presented like a bill for payment. All life in these lower worlds is tied together by millions of threads of karma."

The winter sun sank toward the horizon, leaving a bluish white cast over the fields of snow. A few high clouds graced the western heavens as we hovered over the fields a brief moment before leaving.

"One more thing," said Paul. "The slightest act is recorded in the great Akasha, the ether that composes all life. The Akasha is a record of daily events in the Book of Life that St. Paul spoke of to the Galatians: 'For whatsoever a man soweth, that shall he also reap.' It is the Book of Records that the Lords of Karma examine to determine the just merits due a person at the time of death.

"But the Soul Travelers of ECK hold out to all the path of karmaless action. Thus Soul is free of the Avenging Angel and goes to heaven in the company of the Mahanta, who is lord of every ruler in the worlds of God."

If you would like to try a Soul Travel exercise, here is an easy one that should let you meet Rebazar Tarzs or enjoy a short journey in the heavens of God.

Go back to the beginning of this chapter to the beach story. Picture yourself walking in the sand at the edge of the water. The warm waves wash about your feet, and a light spray from the ocean leaves a refreshing mist on your face. Overhead, white gulls sail silently on the wind.

Now breathe in as the incoming waves wash toward you on the beach. Then, on the outgoing breath, sing *Rebazar* (REEB ah zar) softly in rhythm with the waves returning to the sea. Do this exercise for twenty to thirty minutes every day. After you are skilled at this exercise, Rebazar will come and give you of the wisdom of God.

If you live near the seashore, walk along the beach to get a feeling for the sounds of the ocean. Or imagine the feeling of sand under your feet, the ocean spray, and the many blue-green waters that reach to the horizon. Use your impressions from the seashore in your daily Soul Travel exercise.

You may not ever see Rebazar or another ECK Master on your short Soul Travel journey, but someone is always near to lend a hand, should you need it.

At first, you may feel that you have only met Rebazar in your imagination, but in time and with practice, you will find that he is every bit a flesh-and-blood individual, even as you are.

In my dream, someone in the church had brought a copy of Paul's book, *The Tiger's Fang*, intending to denounce that journey through the vast heavens to God.

3
Our Dreams and Early Religion

Dreams can tell us everything we need to know to get along in this life, but how many people really believe that? If people actually did, the study of dreams would be much more prominent in our society than it is today.

Most of my life I also paid little regard to dreams. My early dreams were of two kinds: the bad and the good. The first were nightmares, and the less they came, the better. Even the good dreams had little to recommend them, since everything in them was topsy-turvy. I usually blessed the deep and dreamless sleep, because in that unknowing state there was a kind of refuge which did not threaten my waking life.

In fact, my recollection of dreams started to flower shortly after I began my study of ECKANKAR in 1967. My desire to Soul Travel had aroused my curiosity about the invisible worlds, and soon I bought a notebook to record any adventure that might occur there.

In time, I learned that the dream state is the home of the Great Psychologist, the Esteemed Prophet, the Noble Sage, the Inventive Travel Agent, the Master Physician— yes, the Great Everything. Dreams taught me to face myself, let me see the future, took me to the heavens of God, and even apprised me of impending illness and where to obtain the cure. During my years in ECK, my respect for the inner teachings of dreams has grown considerably.

Perhaps my early lack of concern about dreams was due to the influence of the church. The first exposure most of us have to religion is in the church into which we are born: the social religion. For many, the church of their birth serves their needs for the remainder of their lives. But others, who chose this incarnation to advance in spiritual understanding, move naturally to a religion of choice: a personal religion. The personal and the social religions are in conflict with each other, and both can vie for the favor of the individual.

This is the battlefield of Soul. Is one to stick with the religion of his birth even though it no longer meets his needs? If one leaves it, can he expect to be hounded by his family, which tries to get him back into the fold? If he has the courage to leave the religion of his childhood and follow a path that is more to his liking, he can be swept by feelings of guilt. Did he do the right thing? Will Christ put him on trial for a violation of faith on Judgment Day?

The fellowship of his childhood church is a karmic union. His withdrawal from that church may indeed cause problems with those members of the congregation who may try to impress upon him the stupidity of his decision to leave. Any subsequent guilt the individual feels will try to work itself out in his dream state.

Replacing a basic system of belief, such as quitting one religion and joining a new one, has a profound effect upon us. We are often tormented by the thought: Have I betrayed my loved ones? Is it their understanding of God that is right? Will I suffer damnation for choosing another master?

The very same questions haunted me when I left the Lutheran church. My confidence in the Mahanta was becoming stronger, but then there were the inescapable relapses into guilt and fear. Guilt is a kind of tax, a fear of having displeased someone whose good opinion of us seems important. For whatever reason, my confidence in ECK hit a low point at indefinite intervals. It was not any failing of the ECK that caused the uncertainty, but the power of my old beliefs launching a new assault when my spiritual defenses were weak. The reason might have been a change in job, a shortage of money, or another problem too large to handle.

Guilt and fear were so deeply ingrained in me that they rarely came to my conscious attention. But they were always there. They made me irritable, frightened, and defensive.

Guilt may come from being made to feel that we have turned our backs upon a commitment to God, our family, a charitable group that expects a donation that is not forthcoming, or an employer who "suggests" we finish a project on our own time but we beg off with a tale about a prior engagement.

When I left my country church in 1970, I submitted my resignation to the elders. After that it felt as if I had drifted into the path of a cyclone: Everybody was bent on luring me back into church, and squeezing me back into my baby shoes. My fight for self-determination left wounds, but within a year's time I had rearranged my life so as to be out of reach of the church members.

This, though, did not put an end to their attempts to "save" me from what they considered to be the diabolic ECK teachings. The congregation held special prayers for me. This was an insidious way of trying to alter my beliefs against my will—a crime against the spiritual law. Their prayer energy began to invade my dreams, which had been awakened through my study of the ECK discourses. Suddenly, on the inner planes, I repeatedly found myself back in church, forced to sit through tedious and stultifying sermons. Sometimes in the night I thought I might scream out in despair against these psychic criminals, these "good" church people.

To ward off these inner assaults, it looked as if I were on my own. But then Paul Twitchell, who was the Living ECK Master during my first years in ECK, began to show up in my dreams. He began to accompany me to church; in fact, he often took me there himself. He did this to purge the beliefs of the church from my system.

One cannot just up and leave a church that has shaped his very thoughts from childhood. There is always a price to pay, if only an emotional one. Such a sudden change can damage one's emotional body. In other words, his aura of protection can be weakened, like a fortress wall breached by a catapult. He is subject to invasion by outside, hostile forces as long as that breach remains open. Paul, the Soul Traveler, came to shore up my spiritual defenses, and this is how he did it.

Time after time he took me to an inner church, to make me face up to my fears about associating with former friends who were fanatical in their efforts to restore me to the church. I had resigned from the physical side of the church, but the same separation from the old ways had to be accomplished in my spiritual life. Paul often kept out of sight during my inner attendance at church services, but before worship was over, he would make his presence known in some fashion that I could well appreciate.

Once Paul took me into the other worlds in such a state of full awareness that I actually forgot that I was asleep and that my physical body was lying in my room in Pasadena, Texas.

During this particular incident on the inner planes, I arrived late at church with a brother. Just as we entered the building, a funeral entourage was leaving it. We pushed through the crowd to get seats two rows from the front, next to the other members of our family. They look pleased that I had come and I knew they were hoping that the sermon would lessen my interest in ECK. Then everything would be back to normal in their eyes, the way it should be.

Disgusted at allowing myself to be caged into another church service, I turned to my brother and said, "Here I am in church again. If I had as much sense here as I do in dreams, I'd just get up and leave!"

The dream was so real that it never occurred to me that I was anything but awake in the physical body.

In front of us was a hymnal rack. Someone had brought a copy of Paul's book, *The Tiger's Fang,* intending to denounce that journey through the vast heavens to God. Eager for something which promised to be better spiritual food than the church sermon, I picked up the book and began to read, thinking: Ah, something ECK to get me through this service.

The setting of this dream experience, which included the funeral, meant that the old way of worship was dead for me. Paul, the Mahanta at the time, was saying that the simple belief and faith of the church were no longer nourishing spiritual food for me. Something new was here to replace this social religion; this, of course, was ECK.

How real the silent world of dreams! On one occasion, an unknown ECK Master spoke to me in a dream of what had once happened to him while he was learning the secret things of God.

This ECK Master met me in a woods in the inner worlds, by the waters of a sparkling brook. The woodland creatures—the deer, squirrels, raccoons, and rabbits—moved within feet of us, showing no fear. The Soul Traveler wore a maroon robe that reached just below his knees. In simple words he told of an experience from one of his travels.

"Each time we go deeper into the heart of God," he said, "our experiences become more awesome, yet also more terrifying. And this is how it must be.

"Years ago, right after I had begun my dream travels, I was on vacation in the South. I decided to explore an underground cavern but soon got lost in its dark chambers. In places, the ceiling of the cave was barely two or three feet high. Terror for life itself could have overcome me at any moment, except that as my situation grew more hopeless and desperate, I began to become detached from it.

"Suddenly my Spiritual Eye opened. Instantly I was outside my human body, and in the Soul form. Here was a new and higher consciousness, completely apart from the physical part of me that groped fearfully in the cavern below. In the Soul body I saw a narrow shaft ahead. Just that quickly I returned to my body.

"I never lost faith, but trusted the ECK to guide my search to find a way out. After some interval of crawling about with no sense of direction, I sensed a draft of fresh air and followed it. It blew from a shaft, or chimney, that indeed led to the outside. At no time did I doubt the ECK, the Holy Spirit, while lost in the underground labyrinth. The experience was necessary for me to come to a higher realization of God.''

With that, the narrator finished his story and left me to ponder its meaning beside this brook in the inner worlds.

The Dream Master, who is the Mahanta, had given me the dream with the unknown ECK Master to convey something important about ECK. The method of teaching used was this story told by the ECK Master. The dream was to assure me of the ECK's protection in any situation, even in what appears to be the most hopeless one. The lesson was given in the form of a story, which the Living ECK Master knows will stick in the mind of the dreamer, if anything will at all.

Dreams can also foretell the future. Six months before my father's translation (death), the Dream Master arranged for an inner experience to prepare me for this event. I had a dream in which my dad announced he was selling the farm and the cows. The dream censor, the part of the mind that acts as guardian for our waking consciousness, obscured the meaning of the dream. The jolt of knowing about Dad's death beforehand might have crushed me.

In the dream, Dad explained that a millionaire from a nearby city had bid for our land. The fact that the dream spoke of a wealthy man indicated riches for Dad beyond his wildest dreams. Even though the land would probably not bring more money than the market value, a millionaire had made the offer. And what greater riches for Dad than to go into the other worlds after a full life on earth?

The dream censor tried to hide from me the fact that Dad would die within a short time, making the farm useless to him. The dream saddened me, and I recall thinking: How long would Dad last without chores? He would not be the first person to die after suddenly losing his reason for living.

True to the dream, Dad died soon after. It was in 1971, a month after Paul Twitchell's death in Ohio.

The single purpose of life is for Soul to cleanse Itself of karma and become a Co-worker with God. All kinds of training aids are provided for It to realize this goal. They include the study of dreams; but even in dreams, one must shy away from any roundabout route to God.

Life has a way of stringing us along. The nonessentials in life use up our time so that none remains for spiritual pursuits. Our backward priorities cause needless lifetimes of reincarnation. But there does come the lifetime when enough of the karmic ties are cut to allow us the freedom to ask: What am I doing here? Our search for truth begins with that single question.

A dream may be the means to teach an individual a significant lesson. One such lesson is to comply with the law of silence in regard to dreams, especially when the information in the dream affects people other than the dreamer. Can we think of a better example than the Old Testament story of Joseph?

Joseph, the seventeen-year-old son of Jacob, was a dandy. He was the youngest son, and his brothers were jealous because of the special favor he enjoyed with their father. To make matters worse, Jacob made Joseph a coat of many colors, which did little to endear him to his brothers.

To add insult to injury, Joseph told them about a dream in which he and his brothers were binding sheaves in the field. Joseph's sheaf arose by itself, and the sheaves of his brothers bowed down in a circle around his.

They said to him, "So you think you're going to rule us, do you?" Humbly, no doubt, Joseph turned his face into his coat of many colors and blushed because they had divined the obvious truth in the dream.

With the insolence of foolish youth, Joseph told them of a second dream. This time the Sun, the Moon, and eleven stars made obeisance to him. When his father heard about the dream, he rebuked his son. The meaning of the dream was all too clear: The family would one day acknowledge him as a royal personage. That was too much for his shepherd brothers, who waited for a chance to put him in his place.

One day Jacob told Joseph to check up on his brothers, who were tending sheep in Dothan. When his brothers saw him approaching in the distance, they made a vow to be rid of him for good.

When Joseph arrived, they stripped off his beautiful coat and threw him into a pit. In the meantime they sat down to eat, to get up the courage to kill him. But then fate brought a caravan of merchants on their way to Egypt. Judah said, "Where's the profit if we kill him? After all, he is our brother. Let's sell him to the traders." So, overwhelmed by brotherly affection, they sold Joseph to the merchants for twenty pieces of silver.

The outcome of Joseph's dream is biblical history. The Ishmaelite merchants took him to Egypt. There Joseph continued to work with dreams, interpreting them first for Pharaoh's servants, then even for Pharaoh. This led Joseph into becoming the governor of Egypt, where he

58

prepared for the famine foreseen in Pharaoh's troubling dream. The same famine eventually brought his family to Egypt in search of food.

When his brothers appeared before the governor, they did not recognize him as Joseph, their brother. In the ensuing conversation, Joseph got good mileage out of the time, years ago, when they had sold him into slavery. But in the end he supplied them with all their needs and more.

The prophetic dreams of Joseph are of great interest to us. He and others like him learned to see the future through their dreams. Such an ability gives hope to a gloomy present, when troubles may threaten to upend an individual's grip on reality.

In addition to opening a door to the future, the dream state is also the instrument of spiritual enlightenment. The Dream Master may use a dream to caution an individual to retain his balance when the illumination occurs. During one of my dream travels I came across a woman living in the inner worlds by the name of Betty Meyers. She shocked her friends one day by declaring, ''I am the God of the Bible, and I wrote it!''

She had entered into the Astral consciousness and was trying to express her feelings of union with the Cosmic Force. This sudden change from her normal sedate demeanor startled her loved ones. Instead of her usual stylish clothing, she had taken to wearing old-fashioned garments. For a number of weeks she was in danger of being committed to an asylum because of this spiritual intoxication. No one understood her. But finally she regained her inner stability and was able to readjust to her home situation.

The dream was a warning that society does not condone behavior too far outside certain boundaries of tolerance. When a person becomes unbalanced and crosses that line, the authorities take him into custody until he is able to resume behavior that is acceptable to society.

Religion, as mentioned earlier, falls into two broad categories: the social and the personal. A church member is counseled by his minister to desire the Kingdom of God, but is not provided a map for the best route to take. Faith is not it. In reality, the doorway to heaven is in the heart, and the Spiritual Exercises of ECK are the key to the secret worlds of God.

There is a quaint little story that when the gods created man they looked for a place to put Soul so that the outer man would not find It except through the toil of searching and growth. Finally, they put Soul in the heart of man, and ever since, man has been looking for, but not finding, the spark of God that he is.

In 1979, a congressional subcommittee held informal hearings on whether to investigate new-age religions. The question at issue was: Can Congress determine the validity of a new religion as opposed to an old, established one?

Several witnesses were brought to testify before the subcommittee and they concluded that no one in America can pass legislation that limits an individual's belief in God. For instance, if a zealot or saint claims to have had the experience of God, who can say he has not—a judge, a scientist, or even a priest? What distinguishes a person who has truly seen God? No single characteristic covers all the different degrees of illumination.

As a matter of fact, hardly anyone ever sees the ultimate God—the SUGMAD—but only a lower manifestation of IT. This is generally the governor of a particular heaven, such as Jehovah (Astral Plane) or Sat Nam (Soul Plane). Whoever sees such a being of light without the Mahanta beside him is likely to emerge from the experience in a state of disruption and unbalance. The Spiritual Traveler can put the person's experience into perspective.

The glory of even such a minor lord as Jehovah will astound an unsophisticated, neophyte traveler. Deceived by his own vanity, he wants to believe he is the Lord's special messenger, because they have met face to face. Immediately he sets out to organize a following.

Now what has all this to do with the dreamer in ECK? The chief difference between ECKANKAR and orthodox, or institutional, religion is the thoughtful attention paid to one's inner experiences in ECKANKAR. These revolve around the Sound and Light of God. The final source of divine knowledge and inspiration is the Kingdom of Heaven within us. It is not in a Sunday morning sermon preached from the pulpit. The Inner Master therefore is the authority for the spiritual man.

The ECK teachings are combined in the Inner and Outer Master. Through the outer teachings the initiate of ECK learns the laws and conditions of the Far Country. Then the inner teachings give him the experience of what the Holy Spirit is doing to make him a greater being. In this we see the joining of our waking and sleeping activities. The dreamer in ECK is forewarned, given insight, and enlightened in his dreams. This merging of one's inner and outer worlds makes ECKANKAR the most dynamic spiritual force on earth today.

It has been repeated so often: A religion must have a leader who can be both the inner and outer master if it is to remain a viable path to God. That was the problem encountered in primitive Christianity at the death of Christ.

The crucifixion threw the disciples into a turmoil as they scrambled to fill the position of leadership vacated by Jesus. For a while the church hobbled along under the exhortations of the apostles, who were a poor second for Christ as the outer master. Then Peter stepped into the breach. His claim to leadership was that Christ had appointed him shephard of the flock. Centuries later, the Roman Catholic church promoted the idea of Peter as the first pope. This was in order to consolidate its own claim to the leadership of Christianity, over that of the church at Constantinople. Peter supposedly was the first to see Jesus after the resurrection. Actually, Mary Magdalene had already spoken with Christ, mistaking him for the gardener. But the church at Rome needed Peter for its historical claim to the line of apostolic succession.

St. Paul was a latecomer among the apostles, but he shone as a missionary to the Gentiles, where the real growth of the new church was to come. He is the principal reason for the farflung Christian teachings; he planted the seeds that made Christianity what it is today. This great man was a problem for the church fathers at the time. He was one of the few influential leaders of the church who had not met Jesus in person. Many of the others had been with Jesus from shortly after his baptism until the crucifixion. In fact, when the apostles met to pick a replacement for Judas Iscariot, the man who betrayed Jesus and later committed suicide, they required that the replacement be someone who had known Jesus when he was alive. Matthias fit the bill.

Therefore, until St. Paul came into the picture, a person's influence in the church depended upon whether he had known Jesus in the flesh.

St. Paul must have been a remarkable man. He came to Christianity with only inner revelations, what the others might have called mere secondhand experiences with Christ. It is true that Jesus had appeared to Paul on the road to Damascus, but that was in Spirit: not quite the experience of those who actually ate and drank with Jesus before Golgotha, the place of his execution.

Acceptance of St. Paul as a church figure wedged open the door for the whole Christian Gnostic movement to follow. This is important history for the ECK initiate because many of those in ECKANKAR today lived during the formative years of Christianity. The problems of the present and future which they will encounter as the vanguard of ECK will be very similar to the prejudices they once faced two thousand years ago as early Christians.

That period of history saw a major quickening of spirituality, and the thoughts and feelings of many today reflect those times. This past, buried in the subconscious mind, appears from time to time in one's dream state. It is also in the unconscious likes and dislikes we carry in the present. Right knowledge can free us from the past. This is why dreams are so important: They lift the latch that frees us from that past.

Essentially two strains of religious thought exist side by side at any given time: belief and experience. The first is of the socio-political religion mentioned earlier. It asks the question: "What is the meaning of life?" The second, a true personal religion, acknowledges: "Experience is the crucible of Soul. What can I learn?"

The early church saw this division between belief and experience in the persons of Peter and Paul. Peter believed, but Paul knew. Peter had some degree of inner experience, such as the Light and Sound at Pentecost, but St. Paul received secret revelations when he was caught up into "the third heaven." He was speaking of himself in the third person when he said, "How that he was caught up into paradise, and heard unspeakable words, which it is not lawful for a man to utter" (II Corinthians 12:4).

The difference in states of consciousness between the two men is the inevitable gulf that still remains today between the Christian church administrator and the mystic.

It is not surprising then to have seen one arm of the church consolidate itself with organization and power, while the other branch despised outer controls. Peter was the forerunner of the authoritarian church leader, while St. Paul was champion for the mystical element in the early church. He was a Gnostic, an adherent of esoteric knowledge as being essential to salvation.

For St. Paul, faith was the starting point. Even the mystic must have faith that his inner feelings are right. But he goes further. He has the courage to study his dreams, to at least recognize they are as important as any outer teaching. The orthodox believer begins and ends with the teachings of the outer church. Dreams to him are childish pursuits, perhaps even provoked by the Devil.

At heart, St. Paul had much the same spirit of inquiry as

did Paul Twitchell, the founder of ECKANKAR. Twitchell told his future wife, Gail, that he himself was like the Gnostics. Like them, he was constantly working with ideas and struggling to become the object of his contemplation.

The Gnostics in the early history of Christianity looked to the same source of creative imagination as do the modern-day students of ECKANKAR. This independence of mind, which the Gnostics retained for themselves as a spiritual right, only angered orthodox church leaders like Tertullian. The issue under discussion was resurrection. Tertullian, speaking for the orthodox mind of the church, insisted that the resurrection of the body was a literal fact. The flesh and blood of the deceased would be the body to arise on the Last Day.

The Gnostic Christians would not bend to such inordinate nonsense. Tertullian branded them as heretics, and the orthodox church came to accept his doctrine of bodily resurrection.

Yet St. Paul himself distinguished between the ''celestial'' and ''terrestrial'' bodies. To the Corinthians, he said, ''Now this I say, brethren, that flesh and blood cannot inherit the kingdom of God; neither doth corruption inherit incorruption'' (I Corinthians 15:50). This is an argument against the bodily resurrection proposed by Tertullian.

Many Gnostics expected a quickening of their creative imagination after gnosis, the enlightenment. But they knew that in order to have enlightenment, it was necessary to have self-discipline along spiritual lines. It follows that contemplation was an inherent part of their inquiry into the esoteric things of God. Those who lived the true Gnostic life contemplated every day.

In contemplation, the mind is stilled by a spiritual exercise. The screen of the mind is blank, untroubled by darting thoughts.

Thereafter comes either the Light or Sound of God, or a

combination of both. This combination may manifest as the Mahanta, or the Dream Master. He meets the individual on the inner planes: in the dream state or during Soul Travel. The meeting is generally on some subplane of the Astral world. This is the beginning of Soul's journey to God; the journey brings self-knowledge, God Consciousness, and the ability to enter the Kingdom of God in this lifetime or the next.

When Soul becomes absorbed into the Holy Ghost, then Soul is a Co-worker with God. It now has the choice of how to serve creation throughout eternity, into the timeless realms.

Everything must be earned in a spiritual sense. There is no free lunch, no matter how much the wretched implore God to pour the Water of Life into their upturned vessels. Faith alone cannot bring one to the Kingdom of Heaven. It must be followed by personal experience in the inner worlds. Self-Realization, which is known as the ECKshar, surpasses the reach of thought.

The enlightened individual may become like the seventeenth-century German mystic Jakob Böhme, a common cobbler who one day was struck by the Light of God. This experience opened his understanding to spiritual knowledge that far surpassed that of classical scholars, who could only boast of mental knowledge drawn from books.

The study of dreams through the Dream Master is really a search to find our own hallowed ground. Perhaps a more typical example of the effects of illumination are reflected in the humble life of Brother Lawrence. His story is briefly told in a wonderful little book, *The Practice of the Presence of God.*

He was born in France as Nicholas Herman during the seventeenth century. Uneducated, he served briefly in the army until his enlightenment occurred on a cold winter day in 1666 at the age of eighteen. It came while he was contemplating upon a barren, leafless tree that would reveal the renewal of life in the coming spring. Such was the simple occurrence that radically changed his life, and he became a Carmelite lay brother in Paris. Brother Lawrence's pleasure was not found in dogma and doctrine, but in entering into direct communion with God no matter how lowly his station or task might be.

The kitchen became his hallowed ground as he scrubbed the pots and pans. Rich in consciousness, he was like the great Tibetan ECK Master, Rebazar Tarzs, a God-Realized being who keeps a sparsely furnished hut in the wilds of the Himalayas. All ground and every circumstance is sacred to the spiritually awakened.

Brother Lawrence affirmed that any piety or spiritual discipline was useless if done without love for God. A little at a time, during danger or the routine of living, we learn to put our attention ever more upon God.

How do we prepare for entering into the God state, or the Kingdom of God? We act *as if* we are already in it. The currents of life will then draw us into the conditions that lead to total awareness. The sustenance of Soul derives solely from the Voice of God—the Sound and Light. The Spiritual Traveler becomes the Inner Master and Wayshower for the individual who seeks the true God beyond all gods. The God beyond Jehovah.

The future is unformed for Soul, which can assemble Its own destiny from among an endless array of possibilities. But It must first learn to act *as if.* This learning begins with the ECK study of dreams.

Over a period of seven years a follower of ECK had a repeating dream on the same subject. Each time he had it, he wondered what its meaning might be. In the dream, Wah Z (the Dream Master) brought a large plate of food to the table where the ECKist was seated. Many other people were also at the table. Wah Z said, ''It's your turn to serve the president of the country.'' The dreamer did as he was directed, walking to the other end of the banquet table and setting the food in front of the president. A white hooded robe hid the face of the president, but despite that, a resplendent light shone from the man.

Finally, the dreamer realized that the dream censor, the subconscious faculty of the mind that tries to protect the emotions of the dreamer from any kind of shock, had substituted the person of the president for Sat Nam. Sat Nam is the great ruler from the Soul Plane who is in charge of all creation from there on down to the Physical Plane.

This dream told the dreamer that the Call of Soul was drawing him to serve the SUGMAD, the true God of all. He had felt the Wind of Change, the lingering breath of Spirit in his dream, through seeing the Light of God from Sat Nam, one of the rulers established by the SUGMAD as caretaker of many kingdoms. The Breath of God, the ECK, should It touch our dreams, begins to create in us a new concept of being.

One time Paul Twitchell took me on the inner planes to an ancient ark church. When we sat down, a long-haired minister with windblown hair, who resembled the medieval paintings of Jesus, approached the altar. The minister turned and asked the few of us in attendance, ''Will it be the Mahanta for you or the Ahanta [the ego]? If the Mahanta, then please conduct yourselves that way.''

I was truly surprised to find reference to the Mahanta, the highest state of God Consciousness, spoken of in this isolated church. This God State he spoke of, the Mahantaship, is above cosmic consciousness and all other such reflections from the Mental Plane. The minister set forth the challenge: How long will Soul remain in the state of self-interest before It surrenders everything of the ego to the Inner Master?

* * *

And so the dream teachings of ECK begin.

A simple method of moving into the higher states of awareness is to combine contemplation and dreams. First, find a quiet place for contemplation. It is our first effort in undertaking a new spiritual endeavor. For a period of fifteen or twenty minutes a day, shut your eyes and put attention upon your Spiritual Eye. This is the spiritual organ of inner vision that is located between the eyebrows, and about an inch and a half in. Look gently at an imaginary screen between the eyebrows and softly begin to sing *Jesus, God, HU,* or *Mahanta. Wah Z* is also acceptable.

Look for a Blue Light upon the inner screen. This is the Light of God. There may not be this Light, but you may hear a Sound. The Sound is the other manifestation of the ECK, or Holy Spirit, and may be almost any sound of nature or musical instrument that you can imagine. The Light and Sound, when they appear, are assurance of your contact with the Word of God.

The second part of this exercise is for the dream state. Prepare for sleep by singing one of the words given above. This is to set into motion an affinity with the Sound Current, the Holy Spirit. For a few minutes, sing the word you have chosen. When you are ready for sleep, imagine that you are walking in a park or watching a quiet sunset with someone you love. A loved one can open our heart and dispel any fear. Love is necessary if one is to enter the awakened dream state.

Finally, keep a diary of whatever comes to mind in contemplation or during your dream state. A mutual confidence will develop between your inner and outer selves, and the two techniques above will help accomplish that.

This is how to start the dream teachings of ECK.

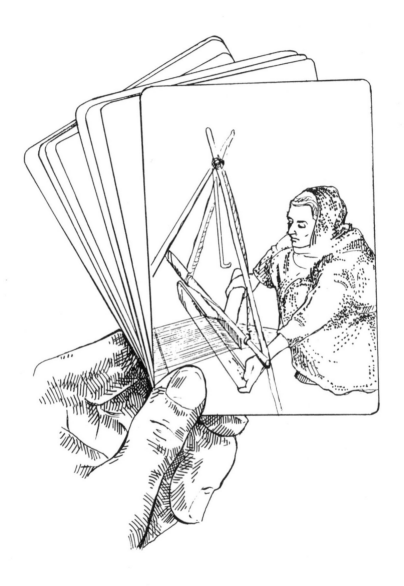

I had grown up with Jesus in the little town of Nazareth in Galilee, some fifteen miles west-southwest of the Sea of Galilee. My family were rug weavers, and my father took the rugs south to Jerusalem several times a year to sell.

4

Land of Distant Memories

Many of us travel to the Causal Plane, the plane of memories, but ironically, we forget about it later. This is the area of memory, and it includes the past, both near and far. The instant we complete any act, regardless of how mundane it may seem, a record of it is preserved on this level of the lower mind.

The entire Causal Plane is thus a warehouse of dead images, but these images take on a life of their own when we place our attention upon them.

To some, the past is more real than the present. There is nothing unusual or wrong about this, unless one spends too much time in the past. For instance, a person who is in the habit of starting a sentence with ''I remember when...'' is on the Causal Plane. The past creates a tangle of inaction, of spiritual immobility; Soul's real seat of operations is action—in the here and now.

The mind, when it shuts out certain scenes from our past, is under the control of the censor. This censor is the function of the mind that guards us from shocking memories that might shred our lives into pieces which won't fit together again. The censor is a critic that inspects, then cuts out an offending memory, the way an editor amends a manuscript.

All this editing and filtering of memories is going on in our minds every minute. Although Rebazar Tarzs had saved her from tragedy, the child mentioned in an earlier chapter forgot his role in her rescue until many years later, when she was a grown woman. The censor had judged this experience too traumatic for a child and had repressed it until she was an adult.

Another case of the censor blocking a memory which might trigger an emotional backlash is the following story. This near-death experience awoke a woman in the Soul body.

In the mid-1970s, this individual went to the beach with a group of friends. They played in the shallows with a beach ball, but sometimes the waves coming toward shore were so strong that they covered the swimmers' heads and bodies. Then the swimmers had to paddle back to shore to regain the ankle-deep water.

The waves came stronger, faster, and higher. Then an enormous wave rolled in from the ocean. Someone in the group shouted, ''Let's get out of here!'' That was the time she did not come up: Instead, she was flying serenely toward heaven in the Soul form.

She was having the time of her life, an adventure in the Soul body. She felt happy, free, and pleasantly relieved of all cares. In the Soul body she enjoyed a 360-degree viewpoint, so while she flew toward heaven, she could also see her friends, like a cluster of ants, on the beach below, wondering if she would ever come to the surface again.

The next instant she was back in her physical body, standing in the ocean with arms spread wide, smiling at the others. They said, ''You were gone a long time. Are you OK?'' ''Of course,'' she said; she felt fine. Later she and a companion swam in the ocean with an inflatable raft as if nothing unusual had taken place. Her swift return to the body had utterly erased any memory of the Soul Travel journey.

A long while later she made a visit to her sister, who had

first introduced her to ECKANKAR; they were to meet two other people to talk about ECK. In the middle of their conversation she was suddenly back at the beach, in the Soul body again, where she relived the episode of being out of her body and flying toward heaven.

This time she remembered the whole incident; she was on the Causal Plane, in the hall of memories. There was not the least suffering while her body drowned, nor did she feel the pain of a struggle for air. But the fact that she had reentered her body was matter-of-fact proof that it was not her time to leave this world.

The censor had reviewed her original Soul Travel experience and had deemed it too shocking to show her then. The memory was stamped "Top Secret" and filed in a drawer in the Akashic Hall of Records. Years later, when she had a better grasp of life through ECK, the censor released the file to her conscious mind. By then she had the awareness to see the connection between her experience and Soul Travel.

Past-life recall is an interesting feature of ECKANKAR, and individuals are often startled to learn that they carry the past with them on their shirt sleeves. The Civil War buff was almost certainly in America during the tumultuous 1860s. The war left such a scar that it now comes to the surface as a deep-felt interest in Civil War history. A child with a passion for model airplanes might well have been an aviator in World War I or II, or a starship commander from Atlantis. Someone with a grudge against a certain church or country for no reason may once have been a victim of their religious or political persecution. An ailment without a known cause, such as a chronic neck pain, may tip-off a person that he was once hanged or beheaded.

The Causal Plane corresponds to the part of the mind where records of causes are kept. A mystery writer like John D. MacDonald touches the Causal Plane on a regular basis but probably does not think of it that way. His character stumbles upon a trail of circumstances that leads to a crime, and as the story moves forward, the plot develops twists and turns. One thing leads to another and ultimately the main character is in the middle of a life-threatening crisis. He studies a string of isolated clues that he must put together. His reflection upon the facts in the case takes place on the Causal Plane, where the Causal mind sifts through the evidence at hand and reaches a conclusion that solves the case.

The past is a take-off point for many authors of fiction. Mark Twain, the renowned American humorist of the last century, was familiar with *Morte d'Arthur,* Malory's fifteenth-century tale of Arthur and the Knights of the Round Table. In the dream state, Twain did more research on the Causal Plane and ended up writing *A Connecticut Yankee in King Arthur's Court.* Twain spiced up King Arthur's sixth-century England with improvements from his own nineteenth century. He introduced to the ancient kingdom such inventions as bicycles, electric lights, telephones, and the like.

These are two illustrations of writers tapping into the Causal world to create story ideas. But the past is meaningful for yet another reason: It tells why our lives are what they are today.

Whenever we have strong loves or hates, it means we have drawn the past into the present by agreement. The past is old emotions collected and gathered around us like keepsakes. They appear to us as family members, friends, and enemies; our past thoughts and actions even shape our physical appearance, our character and temperament. The cause for everything that occurs in our life is chronicled on the Causal Plane, and we are a reflection of that journal.

Soon after learning of Soul Travel, I dreamed of a past life of about 10,000 B.C., after the last of that all-but-forgotten continent of Lemuria had succumbed to earthquakes and volcanoes, and had sunk into the Pacific. My reincarnation was a century after the final disaster, and my hunting range was on the West Coast of America, in what is today southern California. This dream explained my strong urge in the early 1970s to move back to the same area. The rolling hills of Laguna Beach, California, awoke pleasant memories of the gentle terrain of lost Lemuria. But Lemuria's hot and muggy climate had been host to gigantic insects, which were a decided nuisance.

Soul is drawn again to the people and places of Its past. And not surprisingly, the karmic group It rejoins repeats the same old errors in a new setting, for history repeats itself due to a human mind that is a clean slate upon rebirth and does not remember past mistakes.

The dream was of me as a simple wanderer who walked along the edges of a great marsh that had been dry land before Lemuria's destruction. Most of North America was yet swampland, except for chains of islands that reached south to the firmer soil of Mexico, and to Central and South America. Dressed in light skins, the wanderer looked to gather wild rice from the marsh, but he needed a boat or a crude raft for the harvesting. While he made a search along the shoreline for driftwood to build a raft, two savage animals, like wild dogs, bounded toward him, intending him for a meal.

Springing into the low branches of a tree, he straddled a limb, his feet safely out of reach of their snapping teeth. The wild animals settled down at the base of the tree, content to wait for him. Studying his plight, the man broke off a sturdy branch and fashioned a club. He dropped to the ground between the savage dogs. They attacked him, and he killed them with vicious blows.

The threat to his life ended, he skinned one of the animals with a sharp stone knife and ate the meat by his campfire. All the time he studied the wild rice in the nearby marsh, planning a way to harvest it. Rice was handy food on a journey, for a traveler could chew a little of it and swallow the juice for nourishment.

This rather commonplace memory of a past life was nonetheless exciting for me. The Spiritual Exercises of ECK had unlocked the Causal Plane records; the Inner Master was letting me have experiences at a rate I could handle, a rate which at first was very slow indeed.

When I had absorbed the spiritual impact of seeing this past life, Paul Twitchell showed me an even earlier one. It involved my Lemurian family, which also became my family in this current lifetime.

"Your problem *then*," said Paul in contemplation, "was too much honesty."

It was news to hear that there could be such a thing as too much honesty. After thinking it over, the problem seemed rather to be one of ignorance—of the law of silence. The old saw is: Might makes right. If someone has power over us, we had better consider well our criticism of him before speaking. That was the lesson to learn from this second instance of a lifetime with my present family. Paul was to open a window to the Akashic Records for me, and here is how it all came about.

It was winter; I was home on the farm after my hitch in the service. Bitter winds swept our old farmhouse, stirring chilly drafts even inside. Evening chores were done. I stretched out on the living room couch to watch television, but was really watching Dad in the brown rocking chair. He was asleep most of the time, his jerking at regular intervals barely keeping him from toppling onto the floor. His antics left me on edge, unable to concentrate on the TV program.

Watching TV until ten o'clock was mainly to please my parents, so they wouldn't think me odd. They recalled the years when I had watched TV until one o'clock in the morning. To them, *that* was normal. Now their major worry was this: He's twenty-seven and still not married.

A spiritual scientist by nature, I wanted privacy after chores to run experiments on new Soul Travel techniques. My laboratory was my unheated bedroom upstairs. It took an iron will to even go up there. There was no central heating, not even insulation. A tiny thermometer on the dresser by the bed often read in the neighborhood of forty degrees Fahrenheit. Because of the danger of fire, a space heater was only plugged in during extremely cold weather.

It took awhile to get comfortable on the floor by the bed to do the spiritual exercises. Besides long johns, flannel pajamas and a scarf about my neck, I generally wore a long bathrobe. On top of that, two heavy blankets from the bed provided a hooded cocoon to keep the warmth in; after that, contemplation.

My motivation for doing the spiritual exercises while an airman in Japan was to learn Soul Travel, to find a way to visit home without being Absent Without Leave. The military has precious little patience with AWOL soldiers and puts them in places like Ft. Leavenworth prison. My only ambition during military service was to get back home to the farm.

But when I got home, life on the farm turned out quite different from my expectations. This is by way of introduction to a past life in Lemuria: then my family was the same as now, and all the problems of that past life came right into the present.

Dad had struggled for years to make the farm a success and turn a good living for our family. But he had once trusted a building contractor who cheated him out of a large sum of money. The shock of the heavy financial loss blunted his enterprise, and the farm suffered as a consequence. Whenever possible, he excused himself from milking to spend the evening at a tavern. He blocked my conservative plans to turn around the fortunes of the farm: He was the planner; I, the mule. Thus the farm stayed in debt, and I was unable to do anything about it.

Misery forces us to look for a better life. This is why the poor and humble are foremost among those who flock to the Living ECK Master, seeking a crumb of grace, while the wealthy are often too settled in material comforts to want anything better.

The freedom I had expected from Dad, so that I might restore the farm, was on hold. With no hope of improvement, the routine of chores got so burdensome that only the Spiritual Exercises of ECK gave any hope to my desire for growth. If the farm couldn't grow, at least I would. This frustration on the farm gave me the incentive to continue with the ECK contemplations.

The karmic problem in my family that was transferred from Lemuria to the present lifetime involved a conflict between control and freedom. In Lemuria, as here, I was expected to satisfy my father's dreams at the expense of my own. In Lemuria I tried in vain to rally the support of the people to carry out my plans for a better future, but in this lifetime I caught on to the fact that my future depended solely upon my own resources. There was no use trusting the promises of others, for they were likely looking after their own interests.

Yet, in the silence of the inner worlds, I stood tall and free with the Mahanta, the Living ECK Master. Paul Twitchell came in the Soul body this evening to open my past to me by means of the Akashic Records: tally sheets of past lives spent on the Physical and Astral planes.

Besides the Akashic reading, there are two other readings: the Soul and the ECK-Vidya. The Soul reading is a fuller account of past lives spent in all the lower worlds, from the first incarnation to the present. The ECK-Vidya inspects the future through a minute-by-minute or day-by-day analysis that occurs in higher states of awareness. Only the Mahanta, the Living ECK Master has the training to read any of these records for others, although a few ECK chelas do undergo the training to learn to read their own. But the experience that follows concerns only the

Akasha.

Then someone stirred in the room. "Is that you, Paul?" I asked.

"It is," said a firm voice with a Southern accent. A small circle of white light was growing in my Spiritual Eye, a dot that was still millions of miles off in the black reaches of inner space. "Are you ready to study the problems that the wrong kind of honesty can bring?"

Nodding, I put the focus of attention upon the screen of my mind, where the circle of white light had grown to the size of a glorious planet that filled the whole screen of my inner vision. Now a soft buzzing came to my ears, one of the familiar sounds of God that prepares us for Soul Travel. This time there was no sensation of movement: My arrival in the other worlds took but a fraction of a second.

Paul and I were in a golden bubble, and there was no sense of things outside of it. The bubble was a platform suspended in light space, and the only thing that mattered was this great Spiritual Traveler, who was in an old easy chair that he had used a number of times when we met in the far worlds of ECK. In his hands he held what looked like an ordinary deck of playing cards, the backs engraved with a red drawing of an old-time bicycle with a high front wheel. But when he drew a card from the deck and held it up for me to see, it changed into a living scene from the past. In the scene I was both observer and participant: the dual consciousness.

Paul and I stood in the Lemurian countryside under the hot sun. A palace stood nearby, and a town of stone buildings much like those of Palestine, ages later in the time of Jesus. The roofs, however, were of wood and leaves.

"Lemuria was at the peak of its civilization about 50,000 years ago," said Paul. "That was its golden age. By now, however, time had robbed it of its vitality, and the self-direction of the people had given way to a monarchy. This life took place in the last part of that great golden age: an iron age, a minor cycle of the greater one.

"Early on in Lemuria there was no royalty. ECK Masters like Geutan and Dayaka gave direct spiritual guidance to the people. As the land went into a decline of materialism, those with the most ambition and knowledge became the rulers through wile and force. Even though this was the golden age of mankind, it was only relatively so. The ECK Masters went into hiding because of persecution by the kings and priests, a conflict due to the age-old struggle between love and power."

The scene shifted, and we were inside the royal chambers of the palace. The king was in an argument with a soldier who had the bearing of an officer. The king's rage was awesome, but the soldier stood his ground. When the king caught his breath, the other dropped well-chosen words into the fray. This excited a new wave of anger from the king, whose face was a red bulb and seemed about to burst.

In the next moment, Paul and I were walking on the hillside. It was a relief to be out of earshot of the shouting match in the palace.

"What was all that about?" I asked.

"You were the soldier, a captain," he replied. "The royal family was grooming you to be a general in the army, to consolidate its position. The king was your father and main antagonist: your father also in this life.

"There were already hot spots of disharmony among the people at the end of the golden age, although this was the height of this spiritual civilization. The army was created for protection against hostile tribes, to keep order in Lemuria, and for the protection of merchants on trade routes to China, to the Americas and further east.

"The royal family was making a bold bid for control of the army, and you were to be a part of this plan. If you had stopped a moment to consider, you would have seen the folly of a confrontation with the king. His vicious temper made him blind to the fact that you were his son. He, like all others of a negative mind, turned power to his own advantage. But you were a headstrong youth and warned nobles in the court of his plans. When word of your betrayal got back to the king, he was furious and looked to remove you as an obstacle to his plans. The opportunity soon came.''

Again, the scene shifted. Paul and I stood in the cool shade of a eucalyptus grove. In a nearby field two bands of soldiers were engaged in a bitter skirmish. Fighting on foot, they used war implements of spears, axes, knives, arrows, and shields of woven straw and thin hide.

At the front of the battle line, the soldier captain of the royal household swung his stone axe. The enemy force wilted before the onslaught of the king's men, but suddenly the tide of battle swung back in favor of the enemy soldiers, who made a last-ditch effort to capture the captain and break the spirit of his men.

But the king had not left his vengeance to chance. At the rear of the king's troops was an archer with orders to kill the captain should he not fall in the course of battle. The assassin fitted an arrow to his bow and sent the shaft into the captain's back. Suddenly, the battle was over. The king's men scattered in retreat. In a later clash, the royal army drove the intruders from their soil, but for the captain the war was over.

Deep grief rocked me as we observed the lifeless form of the captain on the battlefield. Once a handsome man of Polynesian features, he now lay still—only a bundle of wasted and useless matter. I shut my eyes, refusing to watch the battle scene any longer. For me, the war was over too.

Paul placed an arm around my shoulder. ''Look well,'' he said gently. ''If you understand the failure of the captain, you will never have to repeat such a lesson again.''

The field of battle lay several miles south of the palace. Further south, I could see the white smoke and steam of several volcanoes. There was nothing here but the dead and dying under a blazing hot sun. We made our way back toward the palace on a narrow path that hugged a wide stream. The closest ocean beach was two miles east, and I wished to go there to cleanse the battle scene from my mind. Just that quickly, we descended to the beach from a rolling hill that bordered the water.

As we walked along the narrow beach strewn with rocks, Paul summed up this lifetime for me. "Higher ethics are a natural outcome of spiritual development," he said, "but one must still use common sense as to when to speak and when to hold his counsel.

"That incarnation ended unhappily for you, and your family in this lifetime has rejoined you from Lemuria. Due to misguided honesty that made you react to their plans with blind emotion, you came into this life to balance that debt within yourself. No matter what the cause, we are held responsible for keeping a balanced attitude in all things. When we strike out in anger against some supposed injustice, we must answer to the divine law for our acts, no matter what the provocation."

After this experience, Paul gave me a rest. It took a long time to come to grips with myself.

Each family is a tight knot of karma. The members of my family were not aware of Lemuria, nor of their roles in that ancient civilization. Thousands of kings have held the scepter during the history of the world; the scepter gave them the right to wield—and more often, abuse—power. Those who fail as leaders return as subjects in their former kingdoms: unerring justice.

While we, the actors, polish away the flaws in our spiritual roles, the ages roll on like a slow, deep river—purifying Soul.

Although only my father was mentioned in the Lemurian incident, all the members of my immediate family, and some cousins, were there—in the mixing bowl of karma.

Our character parts change in each incarnation: father becomes the baby girl; the daughter, an aunt; and the uncle, his own nephew: son of his sister. The combinations are without end. When Soul graduates from the multilevel school of action and reaction (karma), It is the God-being. Not God—for that is impossible—but the seasoned likeness of God.

My next incarnation with a direct bearing upon this present life was as a boyhood chum of Jesus. That life was the underlying reason for my enrollment in this life as a preministerial student: I wanted to know all about my ideal, Jesus, the focus of my longing for God.

The thin, biting call of Soul had swept like a wind among the dry leaves in my restless heart. Like the seeker in *Stranger by the River,* I knew that somewhere in this world was a teacher who could excite in me a passionate love for God. The problem with Jesus was that he no longer lived in a human body. With him no longer at the helm as a living master, the direction of the foundling Christian church was at the mercy of the relatively dim spiritual lights of his disciples. The august church fathers who came after them were of even dimmer lights. They allowed the secular needs of the church to outweigh the spiritual. The high teachings of a spiritual giant were left in the care of puny midgets.

The Jesus I had known was not the one shown in the church movie I saw when I was seven. To me, years ago as a child, it seemed that entertainment in church, like this movie, might play wrongly upon the good favor of God. Movies and television were fun, the little that I saw of either; would God permit fun in church? Our dentist, who lived seven miles away, had a television set at the time. Once my parents had taken my brothers and me to a Dagwood and Blondie film, but movies or TV were not commonplace events during my childhood. So when the minister made the announcement on Sunday that a film on the life of Jesus would be shown Wednesday night, I could hardly wait—despite some misgivings as to what God might think of a film being shown in his house of worship.

The film was a disappointment. The projector made a loud clicking noise because the cover was left off: The projectionist found it quicker to correct the picture, when it flickered, with the machine open. But the noise and flickering were not the problem. The Jesus on the screen was not a true portrayal of the real Christ; any child could see that.

My respect and love for Jesus were of the purest kind. But this movie showed him walking along dusty roads with bare feet, bumbling fellows dogging his train. This Jesus was a tall, handsome man, but this creation of Hollywood bore no resemblance to my boyhood friend of so long ago. The zealous group with him on the highway was his small band of disciples, who did their best to hold back the crowds that at times pressed upon them to catch a glimpse of the Jews' latest Messiah.

My instincts as a child said, "This is not Jesus." His slow stately gait neither hurried nor slowed for sun or rain. His somber, but peaceful, face was unbroken by any suggestion of humor, as if a smile would be a sin. Only well-turned sayings—sprinkled freely with "verilies," "doths," "ye's," and "thee's"—fell from his lips. A strange way to talk. Nevertheless, the adults in church seemed pleased with the movie.

I had grown up with Jesus in the little town of Nazareth in Galilee, some fifteen miles west-southwest of the Sea of Galilee. My family were rug weavers, and my father took the rugs south to Jerusalem several times a year to sell. A strict Jew, he preferred the roundabout route east to the Jordan River—to get around Samaria, which he considered a land of heretics. From there, he traveled south on the caravan route to Jericho and Jerusalem, and always in a caravan, as protection against brigands that preyed upon any who were so foolish as to travel alone.

Our family was in better financial condition than that of

Jesus, the family of Joseph, which we came to know well. There were fewer weavers than carpenters, and the quality of our rugs was good; they brought top prices in the markets to the south. We therefore enjoyed one of the better homes in Nazareth, a home built around a central court with about ten rooms opening on to it. Several of these rooms held looms and daylight streamed in from two windows in the block walls that could be shuttered against the afternoon sun by linen and skin curtains.

Clustering the rooms around the courtyard left our home cool, because olive and fig trees provided shade in the courtyard garden. Against the west side of the buildings were terebinths, whose thick foilage provided shade from the afternoon sun. A well was fifty paces from our front entrance, and we lived in the wealthy part of town. Our indoor bathroom was supplied with water by underground pipes, a luxury most of our neighbors could not afford. But, then, trade was good.

The home of Jesus was more modest: a whitewashed cube of stone with a single door and two windows. His father, Joseph, did his carpentry work outside under an oak, and when it rained, he continued in a lean-to on the north end of the building. His mother cooked meals outside.

Their roof was flat, like all the homes, but tilted slightly to allow for the runoff of rainwater. Joseph kept his tools in a corner on the roof, and Mary hung wash there during the day. On hot summer nights, the family slept on the roof.

I first met Jesus in the synagogue's primary school, which we both began to attend at the age of five. The rabbi taught us from the Torah, the holy Law of God. He spoke a sentence, and we recited after him as a group.

Jesus was not a religious fanatic. He was a robust, imaginative youth who was a natural leader at game time. One of our games was Romans and Jews, like ''Cops and Robbers.'' A hatred for the Roman occupation forces was instilled in us from youth. We made toy swords from sticks, and our shields came from square scraps of wood in the carpentry shops. Childhood was a carefree time, except for the time required in school.

The apocryphal *Infancy Gospel of Thomas* says that Jesus had already begun to work miracles as a child. The story is that he turned toy birds of pottery into living creatures, but if somebody believes that, he will believe anything. We played soldier, carpenter, weaver, doctor, and sometimes the role of the wicked tax man. We played ball, but threw and caught it, rather than hit it. One of our games of tag was to hit another boy with a ball and he would be on our side, until everyone was tagged by the thrown ball. Then the game was over.

By the age of ten, we could read and write, and knew the essential parts of Jewish history and tradition. When we were thirteen, our families and a number of other families with boys of thirteen, made the pilgrimage to Jerusalem for Bar Mitzvah, our coming-of-age ceremony. I was not present when Jesus confounded the doctors of law in the magnificent temple of Herod, which was still under construction. All the families from Nazareth were on the way home by the time Joseph and Mary missed him from the caravan and returned to Jerusalem for him.

Our ways parted when we were fourteen. Jesus, whom I knew as Yeshua, joined an uncle on a merchant's caravan going east to Asia. Now that I was a legally responsible Jewish male, I went to Jerusalem to perfect my religious studies. Like many Jews, I awaited the coming of the Messiah, a political liberator who was to restore the House of Israel to her place of honor among nations. Messiah, or Christ, did not then have the meaning to us of "Son of God." This Messiah would drive the hated Roman soldiers out of Palestine, and the Jews would find relief from the heavy tax burdens imposed by the occupation army.

My advanced study of the Law of Moses left me restless. I was a quiet rebel against the restrictions of the Sabbath, although I had no idea what customs might better replace them. The spirit of love was absent from my own life, and therefore everything around me was devoid of love, especially religion.

At that time I wore long hair that curled at the sideburns, for this was required by the Law. During the day I wore a coat of linen, and an outer cloak when it got cold at night. I was rather conservative, despite my restless leanings in religion, and generally wore a brown-and-white striped cloak. A broad belt, folded to a narrow strip around the waist, held my coat and cloak close to the body for easy movement, but the belt also had room for a small dagger, coins, and a snack of figs. Sandals were always worn because of the hot, rocky ground.

My family's wealth provided the means for me to live and eat in Jerusalem during my years of religious study. They hoped I would become a scribe, for these teachers of the scriptures were well respected. But my heart was not in that, nor was there a woman in my life to bring the prospect of marriage. My parents could forgive anything if I would just marry, like a good Jewish man, and give them grandchildren.

Instead, I became a part-time tutor, going home to Nazareth for an allowance from my father when times got hard and food was scarce. By the time I passed my twenty-fourth birthday, the family had all but given up on any plans for my marriage. This was actually a disgrace in those times, because a bachelor was considered to be not quite a man. The family is a strong institution among the Jews.

But I was awaiting the Messiah, an anointed king in the royal line of David. Five hundred years had passed since Zechariah had spoken of the coming liberator, but my search for the Messiah was a convenient way to avoid the duties of a family man. I was a person born out of time. Many of the educated had long since given up any serious notion that such a king was really to come.

That was my life: a searcher after truth, which always seemed to slip between my fingers. I looked for truth, not in a book, but in the embodiment of a man. My parents were barely tolerant of my reports concerning the Essenes, whose teachings I had given a glance because Jesus was once their student. My parents had respect for the Essenes as healers, but as a communal group they were outside acceptable society, and my family discouraged any talk of them in their home.

About the time I was twenty-seven, there was a great stirring in the land about a preacher who was teaching in the wilderness. This was John the Baptist, of Essene background like Jesus, who offered a variation of Eastern initiations by the ritual of baptism, an immersion of people in the River Jordan to cleanse them of sin. His sermons about the promised Messiah caught the fancy of the people, and tremendous crowds gathered to hear him preach. He was the man of the hour, because the heavy taxation by the Romans had raised the spirit of rebellion. The people were looking for a leader, the Messiah, to throw off the yoke of their oppressors.

On one of my trips home to Nazareth, a boyhood comrade said that Jesus had returned home to Palestine from his years of travel. He was teaching a message of love, or so the rumor went.

It would have been easy to accept a Messiah of royal lineage, but I knew Jesus as a lowly carpenter's son. Therefore, I had serious misgivings about him as the prophesied Christ. After all, we had grown up together. I had the courtesy not to laugh at my friend, but the idea of Jesus as Messiah was too much to swallow.

Nevertheless, I was at the Jordan River the day that John, whose name was now on the lips of many people in Jerusalem, pointed to a smallish man who stood before him in the water, ready for baptism. This man's hair was quite short for a Jew, and he wore a modest brown beard. When John directed every eye to this man, who someone in the crowd near me said was Jesus, my confidence that the Messiah was someone other than Jesus was shaken. John the Baptist was a respected religious figure, and when he said, "Behold the Lamb of God!"—that counted for something.

Due to my natural reserve, I kept away from the small groups of people that traveled with Jesus in the next few years. I was still looking for the true Messiah, a temporal leader. News of Jesus' miracles convinced me little by little that he was a special person, but today, taking his miracles in perspective, he only used natural healings that seemed like miracles to the inhabitants of Palestine. The average doctor or chiropractor of today, if transposed to the primitive climate of health care then available, would be something of a wonder himself. Jesus did train under the medical doctors of Egypt, and under the Essenes before that. What seemed like miracles to the people was merely the application of advanced medical knowledge, but these so-called miracles stood Jesus in good stead with them, because it lifted him out of the realm of the ordinary in a land overcome with illness and disease.

If indeed I could not accept the claims of his royal lineage, he certainly was a healer: that I could understand and respect.

Events moved along quite swiftly then. Although three years slipped by, it seemed but a matter of months between the time of John the Baptist's execution and the capture of Jesus himself. By now I had become firmly convinced that Jesus had a message of salvation that outshone the law of Jewish tradition that I had grown to despair of. He spoke of love. This was something my life lacked, which I so desperately needed but could not find.

Shortly before Judas betrayed Jesus, I had gone home to Nazareth for more money. All this seeking after wisdom had kept me from steady employment, so the philosopher had to go home for a loan. When I told my family that Jesus was the promised Messiah, they politely ignored me.

It upset me that no one would take this news seriously, but when the day came for me to return to Jerusalem, my father gave me an allowance as usual, which would carry me for several months on a no-frills budget.

Then, in quick succession, came the capture of Jesus, his judgment, and crucifixion. His death was the death of my hopes. I had fastened all my spiritual aspirations upon his person, and when he was so violently shunted from the public eye, it left me with no one to lean on.

In a daze, I went about the city, unmindful of spending my allowance carefully. Soon it was nearly gone. I took an early trip north to Nazareth to my parents' home, but this time they had had enough. My father became violently angry. Thirty-three years old, I had wasted my entire life, brought disgrace to the family by my bachelorhood, and pestered them with all these notions of a Messiah, while living off the family income. "Get on the road!" my father shouted, throwing a handful of coins after me. My mother pleaded with him to relent, but my father had had his fill of me and my religious pinings. I was on my own.

The roads were dangerous to travelers in those days because of robbers. A traveler was safe as long as he stayed with a caravan, but once past Jericho, I went off the main road to sob alone in misery. Three brigands fell upon me, for they had seen the coins in my belt when I carelessly retied it in plain view of others before the journey that morning. This cost me my life and caused much of the karma that led to this present life.

Paul had given me this past life in a reading I had ordered in the mail, and then had followed it up with a look down the Time Track.

That lifetime as a boyhood chum of Jesus was the compelling reason for my decision to become a ministerial student in this life. Then, as now, I hoped for someone to

90

show me a way out of the narrow confines of religion which taught the letter of the law more than the spirit. Then my hero was Jesus, but I could not fully accept him because of our common background. Then it was too late. In this lifetime, I was led by the ECK to Paul Twitchell, the new-age Messiah. He brought to light the forgotten methods of gaining love and truth through the Light and Sound of God.

Then, as now, my family was staunchly for the orthodox way of religion; I was on the cutting edge of spirituality. My mistake then was not recognizing the greatness of Jesus until after his death. But later, I found that Jesus was a man who brought a Reader's-Digest condensed version of the ECK teachings to the people of Palestine. He brought a popular teaching that fit the consciousness of the masses.

The Living ECK Master in Christ's day was Zadok, who served his mission among the Essenes. I was close to truth, but the outer teacher, no matter how great, can only inspire the follower to find the real temple of truth within his own heart.

"The kingdom of God cometh not with observation: Neither shall they say, Lo here! or lo there! for, behold, the kingdom of God is within you," said Jesus in reply to the Pharisees.

Jesus was aware of the Light and Sound of God: Scattered references remain in the Bible. Jesus had told the Samarian woman at the well of the "Living Water." This was the ECK. Jesus told the Jews on the Sabbath day that they had not heard the Father's voice at any time. He spoke of the Sound of ECK, the Holy Spirit.

That life in old Palestine was a part of my spiritual training to accept the Rod of ECK Power in this lifetime. The lessons of Spirit were finely given, yet hard to endure, but Soul is in no hurry to learn the lessons of life. The ages are lost in a moment, and Its joy in the presence of God is complete. Teachers of the Sound and Light pass through

91

many incarnations before they can shoulder their great mission for the SUGMAD.

In conclusion, the Causal Plane is a repository of memories of Soul struggling to reach God Perfection. The past is important in that the lessons that are learned by hard experience do not need repetition, if one will learn from the past. The Spiritual Exercises of ECK are the ladder to this interesting region of memories that speed one on his journey to God. The Mahanta will not let him flounder.

We find that church, once a haven, becomes a prison. And so the old sanctuary must be replaced, and we find a new one: the ECK cathedral in our heart.

5

The Old Stave Church in Norway

The ECK teachings are given to the individual both here and in the Far Country. The Soul Travelers, the Spiritual Masters of ECK, give us the instruction on the inner planes. But they also help us to sharpen our insights into everyday life, giving us priceless advantages in spiritual unfoldment. There is a natural harmony between the inner and outer teachings.

It was during my service in the Air Force that I first became aware of a heavy, stifling atmosphere in churches. For many people a house of God remains a place of solace, as it had once for me.

Moreover, it was while an airman that I first made the connection between this heaviness in church and the same sort of feeling in shopping centers, especially at Christmas. The downward, negative pull of energy in stores always seemed more intense during the holidays. People were in a rush to do too much shopping in too little time, with too little money. Their pursuit of material goods all but choked off the highly touted spirituality of that religious holiday. The negative vibrations inside the crowded stores would tear at me until I managed to retreat outside to the street. The glaring materialism of the holidays dampened any spirit of lightness or joy in me.

About ten years after leaving the Air Force, I took a trip to Norway. By then, I better understood these negative waves of materialism that appeared in churches and stores alike—and wherever frenetic groups of people came together. When the ECK Masters bring us forward in unfoldment in a short space of time, our sensitivity to such negative pressures is more finely attuned than ever. We become incomparably sensitive to things that used to pass unnoticed. It takes time to understand these changes in our perception. We find that church, once a haven, becomes a prison. And so the old sanctuary must be replaced, and we find a new one: the ECK cathedral in our heart.

Like many others in ECK, I spent a goodly number of past lives in and around religious orders. Sometimes it was as a priest or priestess (for we incarnate in both genders), but at other times, simply as a parishioner. The church had been my temple of God on earth. Ever since then, even though I am in ECK, I have retained a strong interest in churches, and especially in the people who look to them for gratification of their spiritual needs.

So it was here in Norway that I, an ECK initiate, went to see a stave church in a folk museum outside Oslo in 1979. Rain had fallen steadily all morning as I rode the bus to the museum grounds. This ancient, rough-hewn church— when compared with the clean architectural lines of the Temples of Golden Wisdom on the inner planes—was like a hut. But it intrigued me. I have spent more than a couple of past lives in northern Europe, worshiping in similar stave churches. This day at the folk museum was like coming home after many years of travel and finding everything smaller and dingier.

The word *stave* refers to the church's construction. Vertical staves, or beams, inside the building support the roof against the heavy weight of snow in winter.

The church was dark and dismal inside. It was a museum piece and no longer a place of worship; this probably added to the feeling of heaviness. No electric lights had been installed. This was to preserve the building as an untarnished legacy for visitors, to keep the church the way it had once appeared to Sunday worshipers ages ago. Carefully I groped my way through the doorway of the dark room.

When my eyes had grown used to the dim lighting inside, I saw that the floor space of the old church was no larger than that of a suburban three-car garage—unexpectedly small. The whole middle of the church was vacant, like a dance hall floor, except for a few well-positioned staves.

The bus ride and the walk through the mud to this church had left me tired, and now I desired a place to sit and rest. Where had the people in the congregation sat? In the near darkness, I clumped noisily across the wooden floor to benches along the walls.

Accustomed to pews in modern churches that occupy the main floor area in orderly rows, I mused half aloud to myself, "What a strange place for the congregation to sit— along the walls!"

At this, an old Norwegian woman glided from the shadow of a stave pillar. A guide, she bore a striking resemblance to a medieval nun of noble birth. She responded graciously to the question I had asked aloud, thinking myself alone in the church.

"The benches along the wall were for the old people and the ill," she said in her quiet voice. "Children were not brought to church as infants. They came when they were old enough to stand with their parents for the entire service."

Even today, during the summer season, I found the church freezing in the damp weather. It must have been a real test of faith for people to brave winter storms in order to worship here with their neighbors. A wood-burning stove off to one side of the empty central floor was plainly a choice location for those who came to church early or ranked at the top of the pecking order.

For some reason, this old church made me think of Christ. When he brought his message, there were no ground-breaking ceremonies for an outer temple. That came later. Then his followers found it convenient to build their own places of worship, and the race to build ever more impressive houses of worship was on.

Time passed; countless interpretations of the Teacher's words abounded. And so did the ceremonies, the dogmas, and the elegance of the meeting places. Somewhere along the line, the original meaning of Christ's mission was lost in the glorification of outer trappings. People now desired to worship a personality, a statue, and to memorize a translation of a translation of a scripture that a writer had put into a letter perhaps thirty years after the death of Christ. This old church set my thoughts adrift to reflect upon the centuries of Christian development.

The stave church had two doors for the congregation's use. This seemed overdone, considering the small size of the structure; a second door was just another place for the winter wind to creep in through the cracks. Two doors seemed lavish for this tiny, but high-ceilinged room. The old woman stepped forward to explain the reason.

"These dry wooden churches were highly susceptible to fire, and the doors were the only fire escapes," she said. "Besides that, each door had a unique purpose. By tradition, the door in back of the church was the women's entrance. That other door, on the right of the building, was for the men. Men and women came in by their own doors, even though they rode or walked to church as a family. The men and women stood apart throughout the service.

"A few churches still follow this old custom today," the little guide said, "but not many at all."

I told her of an identical custom at our country church in the United States. The old generation of husbands and wives also remained separated during the religious service—the men on the right, the women on the left. Although this custom had pretty much died out by the time I was seven, the older people still clung to it. When their children—our parents—grew up, got married, and began to sit together as families, some of the oldsters were hard-pressed to accept what they considered an erosion of true worship.

Here was a case where a religious practice had developed for some unknown reason. Yet the old people tended to adhere to the segregated seating arrangement as an article of faith. But times were changing. Family unity had already, during the generation of my parents, begun to override the old male-female separation. But old ways die hard. Some of us elementary-school-age children were still made to sit in the front rows of the congregation, away from our parents. The girls sat on the left, the boys on the right—divided in the same way our grandparents had been.

In any event, time marched on. The church council voted to abolish the rule of children having to sit in front. The reason was that their mischievous conduct during service distracted the congregation. Despite the rule change, a few of the traditional parents still made their young sit in the children's pews as of old. Dad made my brothers and me sit in front, by ourselves, to the bitter end. He was taking no chances. Making such a change in the old order of things might be breaking the Ten Commandments. But, finally, even he gave in. My brothers and I were able to sit with our parents like the other schoolchildren and not continue to make fools of ourselves.

Obviously, where one sits in church has nothing to do with salvation, but it is curious to see how easily the mind lets itself slip into such beliefs. These beliefs are then promoted to traditions, which still have no bearing upon spiritual unfoldment. Notwithstanding, people will argue about such drivel until the Last Day.

Tradition is the foremost reason for the feeling of melancholy in so many churches. The church building stores such feelings of dead tradition and magnifies them all out of proportion, passing them along ever stronger to those people who will defend them.

A methodical repetition of creeds cannot bring spiritual freedom. Only the Sound and Light of God can do that. Anyone who is versed in the Sound and Light of God feels penned in if duty requires him to spend even twenty minutes in a place—like the average church—that is so devoid of the Holy Spirit.

"Come, let me show you something," said the little guide.

She led me to the front of the church, beside the altar. Built into the wall panels alongside the altar, and nearly hidden from view, was even a third door: the priest's fire escape. He did not want to be left behind in the event of a sudden conflagration. She referred to him as "priest," instead of "minister," indicating that this was a pre-Reformation building.

A troop of tourists tramped and stumbled their way into the little relic church. The sweet nun lady, as I affectionately thought of her, said good-bye. I watched my step while moving over the dark, uneven wooden planks. Leaving by the men's door, I emerged to see the sun shining through broken rain clouds.

The reason the stave church was of such interest to me was that we all carry the past within us. This is true whether or not we believe in reincarnation. The trials and experiences of past centuries color our attitudes today. As a child, I remember having dreams of stave churches like this one. This visit would now let my dreams merge with those memories of past lives and neutralize the karmic link, and so release me.

From the exhibit of the stave church, I went to another building. Here, in the basement, was the Ecclesiastical Room. Through conversations with the guides about these museum displays, the Inner Master was introducing me to the influence of past religions as a compelling force in my life today.

At first, the Ecclesiastical Room seemed stuffy and

uninviting. Displayed in it were old-time pulpits, paintings, and relics. It would not have been surprising at all to see Martin Luther mount the pulpit steps and deliver a thundering sermon against the pope. The past was still very much alive in this room.

The guide, a young Dutch student on summer vacation from a Danish university, was kind enough to offer her thoughts on religion in Norway. Ninety-five percent of the Norwegians were Lutherans, she said. It was her observation that many of the youth were beginning to look elsewhere than the church for spiritual light.

As she spoke, it occurred to me that with the growing spiritual hunger in Norway, even as this once Catholic country had given way to the Reformation, it might someday awaken to a new age of enlightenment with the teachings of ECK. To all appearances that would seem unlikely, but lightning *can* strike the same place twice in a row. Norway had one reformation already under its belt; might it not someday be ready for another?

The university student spoke German, French, English, Norwegian, Dutch—with a smattering of Icelandic thrown in for good measure. In spite of all her erudition, when I brought up the subject of dreams, they were something to be taken soberly, even feared. When I mentioned a way to systematically study one's inner life, she shuddered. Just the thought of delving into the world of dreams seemed like the very whisperings of the old Evil One himself.

I shook my head; it seemed a good time to leave.

The rain had turned into a light mist. Mud made the paths between the outdoor exhibits treacherous. As I walked to the next exhibit, I realized that this visit to the folk museum was the ECK's way of stretching me. What were the lessons of the past? Jointly, my inner and outer spiritual congestion would be broken up within a short time, allowing me to enter into a higher state of consciousness.

Then I headed for an early-Norwegian farmhouse.

101

Approaching its low doorway, I recalled childhood dreams of a past life in Norway about 1600: a harsh life. The low doorway reduced the loss of heat during the bitter winters. The entrance opened into a sparsely furnished room—a general purpose family room which consisted of a kitchen, living room, and dining area. The fireplace was lodged exactly in the center of the room, rather than against a wall as was common in American log cabins.

Beyond the fireplace, against the two far walls, rested wooden benches. There was also a heavy table—very few furnishings to dress this Spartan room.

Across from the door to the outside, on the right, was the parents' bedroom. It was as poorly furnished as the family room. Each room in the house had an air of dark and forboding gloom. This was due, in part, to the two small—entirely inadequate—windows.

The guide stationed in each exhibit was there for the dual purpose of describing the bygone era to visitors as well as safeguarding the property. This guide, another university student, was dressed in a sixteenth-century costume appropriate to the time in which this house was a family dwelling.

The guide shivered on a wooden bench near one of the small windows, hoping to catch a warm beam of sunshine, should the clouds break to let it through. The few rays of sunshine that did slip between the rain clouds seemed to deliver an enormous amount of light and warmth to the room, probably because there was so little of it in the room to start with. The contrast made the light seem stronger and warmer than it really was. Overall, there was too little sunlight to warm the house but for a moment, so the student huddled miserably in a shawl.

These farmhouses struck a chord of memory. Every farmhouse there evoked new memories of the past. And as the past came into the foreground, it paradoxically began to fade away. Because now it could. The Living ECK Master was releasing the lessons of the past; this visit was a fare-thee-well to old karma.

A nearby farmhouse had a guard tower on its roof as protection against any stranger's approach. A freezing young woman there said that the constant cold was always a problem of survival in the days of old. The iciness, it seemed to me, was still the bane of life here. She also cowered from the cold, a blanket drawn tightly around her shoulders. The inside of her farmhouse exhibit had the bone-chilling cold of our farm granary in winter.

"The average adult," she said, in a lilting accent, "reached only the age of thirty; and an old person, forty. Fifty was highly uncommon."

Sobered, I left the farmhouse. The significance of the unbelievably rough living conditions endured by these early settlers made me wonder how they ever found happiness in this dreary climate. My Causal-Plane records later confirmed that my several incarnations here had been ones of desolate misery. The land still displays its raw beauty; but today it is far more habitable than before the harnessing of electricity and the introduction of modern inventions, which have made living there quite homey.

An individual, in most periods of history, was able to squeeze an average of four or five lives into every century. That is, if he came into a new body right after the death of his former one. Many people died as children, but they quickly reentered a physical body a short time later. Each incarnation was to teach them some facet of life that no other lifetime could teach as well. The cycle of reincarnation seems to drag on endlessly for most people, because they would rather not know what is happening to them spiritually.

Perhaps the hardships of the people then were the force that compelled them to attend church. For instance, a study of cycles shows that when the economy is on a downturn, interest in religion swings upward. Although we learn best under adverse conditions, so many of us pray that God remove the very suffering that makes us more divine.

I welcomed this occasion to look at the living conditions of a long-dead people with my outer eyes. But it was the inner eyes that brought forth this understanding: Soul needs every possible experience to become a Co-worker with God.

The sacrifice or pain that is inherent in suffering compels Soul to place Its attention upon lasting, spiritual goals. Soul is to search for the Sound and Light of ECK and become one with them. These two pillars of God stir a quiet longing in Soul: a burning that only the Sound Current can soothe.

Shortly after this trip to Norway, Rebazar Tarzs, the torchbearer of ECKANKAR, came to me in contemplation. He emphasized how one-pointed Soul's striving for God Consciousness must be. Otherwise, how can the individual ever hope to find this high awareness?

"The thief has eyes only to steal," he said. "And such should be the zeal of the seeker after truth. The search for it must be always on his mind, and thus guide his every action."

I found this trip to Norway an expansive journey into my own spiritual worlds. It was one of many times that the Living ECK Master allowed me to expand my consciousness through a blending of the outer and inner realities. Every little thing counts in our striving for the Allness of God.

The real lesson of that lifetime came as I watched the protective shield that my new friends, the gypsies, were willing to throw around me at the risk of their own lives. There was no advantage to them whatever for befriending me.

6

Temple of the Heart

L ove and mercy open us to inner awareness. Yet the
Inner Master lets us make up our own minds about
the next step to God Consciousness.

I once asked the Inner Master, "Are love and compassion the keys to God-Realization?" He said no, then fell silent.

This was one of the methods of instruction he used during my spiritual training. It took the form of a long-running quiz. After reaching a certain plateau of spiritual understanding, I would ask him for a new direction in my unending quest for the supreme state of consciousness. He would give a hint or two, but then it was up to me to find the answers. This approach was more mystifying than that of the Zen masters, but it worked well.

The Mahanta is the foremost Spiritual Traveler in the Order of the Vairagi Adepts. He is the representative of God who can help Soul find spiritual freedom. The Mahanta is the Inner Master, keeper of the secret wisdom. He guards the temple of the heart, disclosing the hidden knowledge to those who dedicate their hearts to SUGMAD.

The holy scripture of ECK, *The Shariyat-Ki-Sugmad,* Book One, says this of him: "It is best not to make contact with the Living ECK Master in the physical but through the inner level, for all comes as the secret teachings from the heart of the Mahanta to each chela under his protection and guidance. This is the inner way and all who come unto the Mahanta shall be lifted up into heaven.''

Masters from other paths release their disciples to the Mahanta when the latter have learned all that their current masters can teach them. The bridge between the former master and the Mahanta is frequently an ECK Master. An Australian woman told of a dream she had had as a child. In it she got a clear look at Guru Nanak, the sixteenth-century founder of the Sikh faith in India. She was only ten at the time and was surprised to see this revered teacher appear and bless her with an upraised right hand. But when she told her friends about him, they ridiculed her.

With that blessing, Guru Nanak had released her from his teaching. About the same time, she became aware of a being around her, especially when she was alone. If she turned her head quickly, she could see this individual for a split second out of the corner of her eye.

At other times she ran around the house looking for this tall man in the maroon robe. Frightened, she confided in her mother, who said, ''Every time you feel this man, shut your eyes and say *Sat Nam* or *Vi-guru.*'' The girl repeated the names given by her mother whenever the man in the maroon robe appeared. But he stopped making his presence known to her after the family moved out of the area.

About five years later she learned about ECKANKAR. It was then that she heard the name of this ECK Master: Rebazar Tarzs. His love and protection had surrounded her and her family in a community where the practice of black magic was common. Her family's beliefs were different from those of their neighbors, and so they were the objects of spells, which were meant to harm them. All this occurred prior to her knowledge of ECK.

The forces of hate are always at odds with love. But they are often masked behind respectability. People who are

108

otherwise fine individuals sometimes feel they have a mission to convert others to their own religion, by whatever means necessary.

A mother was distressed to find that the director of her child's secular day-care center was using religious songs and prayers alien to the family religion. When she lodged a complaint, the director agreed to quit teaching religion. But this promise was exacted only because the school's funding from the state was at risk. It was not made because the director understood the spiritual law that prohibits such an intrusion into another person's psychic space. Even that of a child.

Zealots do not care about the sanctity of Soul's temple of the heart. They feel they have license to push their prayers upon whomever they please. All this is done, supposedly, in the name of the Lord. But how ethical is that, or does no one care?

The Jesuits' motto once was: "All for the greater glory of God!" That was their justification in the Middle Ages, as an arm for the Catholic church, to assail the Protestant reformers. This included attacks against Luther, Zwingli, and Calvin. The Jesuit doctrine of "intentionalism" was used to mean that the end justifies the means. In other words, it gave them the self-ordained right to further their idea of God's will. Any misdeeds on their part received automatic absolution. Many Protestants today are of the same narrow mind as the Jesuits back then.

Such people are spiritually dead. They are in a dazed condition regarding the meaning of life, and so are those who look to them for direction.

Thomas Bracken capsulized this dazed condition of man in his poem, "Not Understood":

> Not understood. We move along asunder;
> Our paths grow wider as the seasons creep
> Along the years; we marvel and we wonder
> Why life is life. And then we fall asleep—
> Not understood.

A truth seeker looks for enlightenment as he struggles through the negative swamp of life. But he runs headlong into this dazed mass of people who cannot accept truth from the heart. The avenue to truth is via the secret science of Soul Travel. Travel into the spiritual worlds, similar to Soul Travel, was fairly routine during the first century A.D. This is when the Gnostics put great stock in the merits of the inner kingdom. But as time passed, the church leaders were increasingly unable to perform the spiritual flights of Jesus, St. Paul, and St. John. Therefore, they outlawed such practices from the early church.

Simon Magus, a contemporary of the original apostles, lived in Samaria. He was a magician and leader of the Simonian faction of Gnostics. It was he, the Bible says, who tried to obtain spiritual power from the apostles with a payment of money. The church leaders charged him with sorcery because he walked on air as Christ did on water. Other reports had it that he raised the dead.

Church fathers also dismissed the miracles of Apollonius of Tyana as sorcery. A contemporary of Christ, but a few years his senior, he came from Cappadocia. This is in modern Turkey. Among the miracles attributed to Apollonius are the plague he halted in Ephesus, the sight he restored to the blind, his dramatic escape from the chains of Emperor Domitian in the hall of justice, and his sudden reappearance a few short hours later to disciples more than a hundred miles distant. He was further said to have risen from the grave and was, like Christ, seen by many people after his resurrection. Eventually he too ascended into heaven.

The orthodox Christians chafed at the audacity of the Gnostics and others who asserted an inside track to heaven. Yet the Preacher says in Ecclesiastes: "There is no new thing under the sun. Is there any thing whereof it may be said, See, this is new? it hath been already of old time, which was before us" (1:9 - 10). There were those in Christ's day who could perform miracles as he did.

Whatever works Jesus once did can also be done by others today. For he said to his disciples, "He that believeth on me, the works that I do shall he do also; and greater works than these shall he do; because I go unto my Father" (John 14:12). In respect to miracles, Apollonius and Simon Magus resembled Christ more than did the apostles, who are credited with only a few miracles among the lot of them.

But a religion hardly survives because of miracles. It must meet the needs of its people for identity with God. So arose the fallacious idea that Soul is destined to become one with God. The correct stance, and that of ECK, is that Soul actually becomes united with the Holy Spirit. This is the ECK, the Voice of God.

The way to the temple of the heart, which is the Kingdom of Heaven within us, is through the Spiritual Eye. Christ refers to it in the Gospel of Matthew: "Strait is the gate, and narrow is the way, which leadeth unto life, and few there be that find it" (7:14). He meant the single-pointed desire for God that outshines any material enticement.

The real spiritual path starts with belief and faith when it comes to matters of the unknown. It then advances until Soul assumes the limitless state of perceiving all things directly by means of the Spiritual Eye.

Agnostics, like Robert Ingersoll of the nineteenth century, rebel at the traditional God who is made in the image of man. A childhood prayer of Ingersoll dances with blasphemy: "Dear God (if there is a God), save my Soul (if there is a Soul)." Yet his search for truth was surely as earnest as that of those ministers in his day who tried to wrestle him into heaven by argument.

The agnostic's search for truth may be as sincere as that of an archbishop. Any variation in the outer practice of their beliefs is simply due to their different states of consciousness. In the eyes of God, one is no greater than the

111

other. What percentage of people in Christendom know this?

How do the Soul Travelers of the Far Country teach an individual who is in training to be an ECK Master? The Inner Master once brought me into his office and picked up a photo from the desk. He was helping me improve my memory for details. This skill is useful for remembering one's journeys into the Far Country. The photo was of no one I knew.

"Study his nose," he instructed me. "Can you describe any distinguishing features to me?"

There was nothing particular about the nose, but studying it more closely, I was able to isolate a triangular shape in one part of it. To the side of that was another geometric shape, an oval.

"Why don't you do that with his whole face," he suggested.

Yet, when the Inner Master covered the man's face and asked for a verbal description from memory, I was at a loss to give one. He had me study the photo again. Although it was immeasureably hard for me to pick up this knack, I knew the ECK Masters were expert at this sort of identification. It was a method of training the mind's recall of important information.

In spite of my difficulty in learning this, the Inner Master never chastized me for stupidity. This demonstrated the great amount of patience which the ECK Masters employ when showing students unfamiliar disciplines. That patience would be the very thing I would need later as the Living ECK Master. It meant bearing with others when they did not understand something the first or second time around.

Thus my memory was sharpened each succeeding year I was in ECK. And the trials of learning were quickly forgotten when inner experiences, such as the recollection of past lives, came as a result.

The ECK studies bring a deep perception to past-life experiences, which show us shades of our likes and dislikes from a spiritual viewpoint. Some ECKists train themselves enough to glimpse a snapshot of their Akashic records. Only a few care enough to really examine the past, which contains the conditions that bother us today or tell why we have built our lives in a certain direction. After all, the past is only a series of dead images. Simply to view the past for entertainment is hardly worth the trouble of learning the ECK-Vidya, the ancient science of prophecy, which also takes in past lives.

But I had a pointed curiosity about the connection between my past and present, and so developed a series of spiritual exercises to help me learn the ECK-Vidya.

During a lifetime in ancient Atlantis, I developed a taste for the simple life, even though I was born in a house of minor nobility. That lifetime was not marked by any outstanding accomplishments. I had already learned to shun vain and jealous nobles, thus safeguarding my life. Intrigue in the royal court was an ongoing concern, but even more than that was the danger of invasion by warlike neighbors.

I was a diplomat stationed in the city which was the capital of Atlantis. The government house that I was assigned to was colossal, filled with many endless corridors such as are found today in the National Security Agency in Maryland. One day an office girl, walking along one of the remote hallways in the first basement, suddenly gave a scream. Raiders were pouring into the enormous building through the ground-floor entrances and windows.

In that life I was a red man, tall and muscular, about six feet in height. During the first moments of confusion, I bolted down a short flight of steps into a remote part of the building. In this basement, where a hill sloped down sharply outside at the far end of the room, was a forgotten entrance that had been boarded shut long ago. I was able to jar open the top of the entrance with a flying kick. The small opening was just large enough to squeeze through. Running blindly into the night, I sought shelter in the rugged countryside that surrounded the government building that I now fled.

Quickly I stole through the bushes along a ledge overlooking the valley below. The sound of a tumbling pebble disturbed the night, as if accidentally kicked along the ground by a careless foot.

Two enemy scouts, looking for fugitives, melted out of the darkness on a ledge directly under mine. Quietly I dropped behind a scrubby bush that jutted over the ledge. One of the soldiers gave me a bad scare when he ran a step or two up the side of the ledge that concealed me, grabbing at the very bush behind which I lay hid. But he lost his grip and nearly tumbled off the ledge below, as he tried to catch himself. That seemed to curb his interest in scaling my small ledge to use as a lookout post. The two soon rustled off into the night, leaving me shaken and wondering where to hide before the break of day.

After stumbling aimlessly in the dark for some time, I came upon the tiny village of a gypsy tribe. One of the villagers guessed my predicament. He lent me an old cloak to cover my well-made clothing, which the enemy would have quickly identified as belonging to a government official. A crude knife made of hammered metal was slipped into my belt. The old man put a jug of alcoholic beverage in my left hand, a crude sack in the other. My disguise was that of the tribal drunk, an interesting but harmless specimen of humanity.

Shortly thereafter, the sound of hoofbeats broke the silence of the night. A band of enemy soldiers rode up to the main campfire and demanded news from the gypsies concerning any strangers in the area. Since I could speak neither the language of the gypsies nor of the enemy, the drunkard's disguise was quite fitting. I clung to the

114

shadows, away from the fire.

One of the soldiers stepped out of the dark behind me and seized the sack that I clutched in my right hand. The sack held a few rags of clothing and bits of food. To his halfhearted questions, I responded with the slurred phrases of goodwill that one might expect from a drunk. He could make no sense out of my babblings but was assured of my harmlessness. After the soldiers had gone, I thanked the gypsies who had saved my life.

When morning came to this far world in time and space, I studied the countryside, the sights impressing themselves upon my memory. Peasants were busy harvesting grain while other people brought in ripe fruit from multicolored, heavily laden trees. The sky was a crystalline blue, and powder white clouds sailed lazily before a brisk, cool wind.

The enemy's attack had caused no hardship for the peasants. The invasion was intended exclusively to overthrow the government. The laborers were not to be bothered.

I joined the gypsies, and several years later I was able to repay them for saving my life. A swamp dinosaur, light green in color, suddenly emerged from the marshland in search of food. It stood just under fifteen feet in height. As it was about to attack a gypsy child at the water's edge, I was able to distract the creature, beating it with a heavy staff. When the child had fled to safety, I then killed the dinosaur. It belonged to a species which the natives had thought extinct for generations. They expressed a great deal of wonder at the carcass.

Later they honored me for that act of heroism. But the reptile had been easy to destroy because its movements on land were slow and ponderous.

During that lifetime I worked on fate karma, over which I had little control. The nobility was my birthright, which had gained me a comfortable position in life as a diplomat. However, the real lesson of that lifetime came as I watched the protective shield that my new friends were willing to throw around me at the risk of their own lives. There was no advantage to them whatever for befriending me.

With them I enjoyed travel and freedom. Outside of being displaced from my royal life by the invasion, the remainder of that lifetime saw few complications. It was here, among the gypsies, that I came to appreciate the simple pleasures of living.

Some people in ECK do not care to see the past. It takes a great deal of discipline to achieve the inner vision. Even then, results are not certain unless one fixes his spiritual vision upon the Ocean of Love and Mercy, which is the home of the God Force.

Fate karma is a debt which the Living ECK Master seldom alters for the chela, although he will help with both reserve and daily karma. We would like to imagine that we have passed all the big tests of Soul in previous lives with flying colors. Too often, however, the opposite is true. At some time in their thousands of lives on earth, most Souls participate in crimes as vile as those committed by the Nazis in the death camps of World War II.

Payment for such misdeeds always comes due. And when an individual, whose karma has come home for payment, pleads with the Living ECK Master to lift the suffering, it will seldom be done. The Master's first concern is for the purification of Soul. However, most karma will resolve itself during the lifetime in which the individual takes up the path of ECK.

As a sidelight, the Master once showed me how to make less daily karma. He stressed the importance of words in everyday speech. Comparative words such as "almost," "nearly," and "pretty near" used too often make us seem indecisive to the people we live and work with. I began to substitute more direct speech. The overuse of demanding words such as "should," "ought," and "must" belong in the vocabulary of a person who desires control over others. People sense that and shy away away from him. That aversion is karma. Thereafter I began the process of learning how to recast my sentences along simpler, more direct lines.

But such modifications as better word selection are really cosmetic changes. Daily karma is resolved best through this one simple change: Say and do everything in the name of the SUGMAD, the ECK, or the Mahanta. Then your life will begin to turn around for good.

Karma of any kind is fed by the five passions of the mind, but mainly by the factors of ignorance and greed. The corrective for these conditions is knowledge and charity. The mind of man, controlled by karma, wants to acquire property and renown; the spiritual man wants nothing more than to serve God. There is a transition between the life of taking to that of giving. This process begins at the First Initiation. It lasts however long it takes one to learn what it means to live the life of service to God in mind and heart. It is at this point that the tables turn in favor of Soul in Its relationship with the Holy Spirit.

A student new to ECK may gorge himself with everything of the spiritual works that he can find—while giving little or nothing in return to life. His joy in finding ECK is such that it astonishes him. He senses that It is truly the way home to God that he has searched for so long. His enthusiasm runs wild, though. He craves to satisfy his mental appetite by reading every ECK book and discourse he can lay hands to. The consequence is often a fleeting reaction against ECK.

The reaction may actually cause nausea. He trembles at the portal of the secret knowledge, wondering how ready he really is for these ancient teachings of ECK. Doubt seizes him. He may even desert the path, repeating the mistake of a previous incarnation. The Mahanta, the Living ECK Master watches all this from a distance. He hardly will interfere with the chela's decision to stay or go. The choice is entirely his own. The chela alone must choose what path to select for returning to the Kingdom of Heaven.

Let's say the individual finally does overcome his doubts and chooses to go through life with ECK. Now comes the question of how successful he will be on the path. Attainment in the spiritual life depends upon much the same qualities as does achievement in sports. A youth who plans to try out for the basketball team in autumn will spend the summer touching, dribbling, and tossing the basketball until it becomes a part of himself. The same is true of a football player. In fact, a college coach may have a player carry a football around campus for a week—to make the player and the football one—especially if the player's error cost the team a win in the last game.

It is commitment like this that is also needed to learn Soul Travel. The methods are outlined in the ECK books and discourses, but the motivation to succeed in the spiritual works can only come from the individual himself. Self-discipline, not idle wishing, commands results.

For my part, I did everything possible to become conscious of my travels in the spiritual worlds. And it paid off. Paul Twitchell once said, "To learn a subject, teach it." Thus, if I was uncertain about an aspect of ECK, the Inner Master put me on the hot seat. Although I was not always cast in the role of a teacher, he did make me defend my position. This served as well to align me with the Sound and Light.

Early in my ECK studies, I wavered back and forth between the authenticity of the Bible and the reality of the Living Word, which is the Living ECK Master. Once, in the dream state, I slipped into a church service in disguise. The minister arrived late. Finally, he stepped into the pulpit and mocked up an emotional outburst of despair. Shouting, he accused me of causing my sister's damnation because she had left his church for ECK. Then he closed the Bible and dramatically threw it over the heads of the people, into my lap.

But when the Bible hit my lap, I immediately jumped up and threw it on the floor. "The Bible is dead!" I shouted in response. This caused an uproar in the church.

The preacher hurled barbs at me while I stalked down the aisle without a word, heading for the exit. After each of his verbal attacks, I stopped and countercharged that each Soul must look again to the *Living* Word, the Living ECK Master. "Judge for yourselves," I said to the congregation. "You are being deceived by a dead teaching." It seemed they had already guessed that. I was merely voicing their unspoken thoughts for the minister's benefit. After all, did he ever tell them that the Sound and Light of God are needed to attain spiritual freedom? Otherwise, what are they for?

Awakening from this experience, I found myself stronger in Spirit. The inner experience had spared me the unpleasantness of such an encounter in the outer world, while the Dream Master's aim was still accomplished: to have me stand on my own feet and speak up for truth.

The temple of the heart is our spiritual consciousness. All we ever need to know is already within us, but it takes the right approach to tap into the information. That includes spiritual preparation.

Prophecy, or seeing the future, holds a powerful attraction for us. But what good is such a vision if the conditions it reveals are too far beyond our present understanding? When the mind is unable to grasp it, then its significance is lost.

In my own life, I had a preview of my first wife and her family in the dream state during my junior year in high school. The dream made no sense when I tried to understand it the next morning. That part of my future was completely outside the reality of a high school student in preministerial training. My concerns then were in trying to pass my tests in Latin, German, biology, algebra, and religion.

The dream censor concealed this dream from me until years later, when I discovered it while researching the Time Track. A record is filed here of every past event. Details of the original dream had been given so clearly that it was possible to distinguish the individual voices of teenagers who were now my nieces.

When we are on top of life, we feel little need for the inner teachings. But when things are rough, there is no better place to go than to the temple of our heart. Here the Mahanta meets Soul. His guidance often comes as a knowing. In any given circumstance, we are left with at least one of two alternatives: advance or retreat. Yet it may be hard to tell what the Master is trying to tell us, and we wrongly suppose that we are left to our own feeble resources. Actually, he is right beside us every single moment of our lives, to offer us protection. He often gives us guidance in the subtle form of knowing, if we could only learn to hear him.

During the early weeks of my first marriage, my wife stayed in Las Vegas while I drove to California to find work. She wished to finish a two-year commitment of service in the ECKANKAR International Office that was to end in two months. Then she planned to join me on the West Coast.

My job hunt went poorly. Finally, a week before I was to catch a bus to Las Vegas and bring my wife to California, a printing company in a coastal town hired me. Nearly all of my first paycheck was set aside to rent an apartment. The former occupant was still moving out when the landlady showed the place to me.

The pace of events so far in our marriage had been fast, stormy, and tiring. This was our second home in two months of marriage, and half of that time had been spent apart.

The bus ride to Las Vegas seemed to last forever. My wife met me at a casino bus stop, near our mobile home. Everything she owned was in her small two-door automobile; the car was packed to the ceiling. A brake job for her car the week before had used up any money that might have gone toward a trailer. But at least we had confidence in the roadworthiness of her car—or so we thought.

As we pulled out onto the road to begin the long journey through the desert, I began to have misgivings. The car was loaded so heavily that it rested on its axles. The overload provided no cushioning from the shock absorbers: dangerous, but we would be extremely careful. It was as a Latin professor had long ago intoned in high school, "Necessity has no laws."

Halfway to Barstow, California, a desert city in the middle of nowhere, the car's brakes failed. Weary hours later, in Barstow, I downshifted and eased into a service station.

"I'll check the brake lines," said the mechanic. "Why don't you folks just wait in the coffee shop? It'll be at least half an hour."

With misgivings, we did as told. And lunch did sound good, especially since if we did not eat now, there might be no money after the brake repairs.

After lunch the manager gave us the bad news. The brake job done in Las Vegas a week earlier had been done wrong. The repair would cost exactly the amount of rent money in my pocket. But even one brief meeting with my new landlady had convinced me she was an unbending individual. Especially when it came to tenants with hard luck stories instead of cash on rent day. She was renting the place for profit, not charity. So I knew that the money in my wallet had better be in her hands by nightfall, or my wife and I could look for another home.

I was torn; it seemed the rent money was on a trading block. The side with the best argument would get the jackpot. The mechanic wanted the money and only needed my OK to proceed with the repairs. But our dour landlady had been promised the money for rent the night we arrived.

Choices in life sometimes appear to be no choice at all. This was such a time. Common sense said, "Fix the

121

brakes! Live moment to moment. What good is money if you have a wreck?'' My next paycheck was a week away, and no more rent money would be forthcoming before then. If we could just get home, I could drive my own car, which was parked in the driveway.

So I went to the temple of my heart to pose the question: stay or go? The Inner Master said, ''Go! I am always with you.'' We hoped so. It would take more than luck to survive the Orange County freeways during rush hour without brakes.

The service-station crew watched in disbelief as we climbed into our car to continue our journey. The backseat was packed right up to the ceiling, the console between the front seats was jammed full of odds and ends, and the floor on my wife's side had food and drinks for the road. The car was snug, like the cockpit of a jet fighter—and just as lethal.

Driving to Orange County in an overloaded car without brakes was a nightmare. I paid strict attention to the Inner Master's warnings: ''Slow down—fall back—downshift— watch the hill!'' Several miles from home I missed a turnoff. This added thirty more miles to an already exhausting trip.

We arrived completely spent, but also with a sense of wonder in having reached home at all. Our landlady wrote out a receipt, never guessing how dear the money that we handed her for rent was. To her, it was just a return on a capital investment. But we had risked our lives for it. This was one instance where the Inner Master saw me through what could have been a catastrophe.

The SUGMAD is the God of Love, but this does not mean that the weak shall find IT. The wisdom of the ages is hidden in all corners of the world, yet it takes the spiritually awakened to retrieve the crumb of blessing from the lowliest of places. It is where only the humble think to look.

* * *

Although Bibles of all cultures hold some value for the seeker, they are only stepping-stones to the temple of the heart. Written scriptures, though held as unshakable truths, are subject to conflicting interpretations by an endless string of scholars who may warp truth to fit their needs. A scripture fails if it cannot lead one to the Kingdom of God. This kingdom is within our own state of consciousness. It is not off in remote space, but here and now.

All genuine men of God have taught that the Kingdom of God is within us. Not a material empire of jewels or diamonds, it is a region of Sound and Light where Souls of awesome splendor live. That is heaven.

People who pursue phenomena will completely miss the subtleties of ECK. Many ECK initiates have surpassed the orthodox saints in exploring the heavenly worlds. The initiate's spiritual stature is hidden from the ordinary person because the true ECKist is quiet in the conduct of his spiritual life.

There is an interplay between the inner and outer life. An outer experience may spark a meeting with the Inner Master, who tells us how to handle the problem the next time it arises. When I was a supervisor at the ECK Office, the Inner Master came in the dream state. He said he wanted to build some confidence in me. ''This concerns money—'' he started to say. ''Oh, did I say money?''

Thinking he had misspoken, I graciously said, ''We can ignore the word 'money.' '' It seemed he had been ready to offer me a raise in salary. To my chagrin, he asked, ''Were you late for work yesterday?'' I nodded glumly.

''Tardiness is money, you know.''

''Yes,'' I said, ''but there were circumstances. The bus driver drove right past me at the bus stop. In fact, three buses went by like I wasn't there, so I had to walk to work. That's why I was late.''

Instead of the expected sympathy, the Inner Master said,

123

"Then I'd report the driver if he is unreliable."

Another ECK Master was also in the room. He broke in. "Here, let me show you how to stop a bus!" He mocked up a scene of him waiting at a bus stop. When the imaginary bus approached, he waved his arms wildly, shouting jovial epithets like this: "Stop and pick up this dirty old one!" The ECK Master's audacity made it certain the driver would stop.

The ECK Masters will simulate anger or create a scene, as just mentioned, to stir some response in a student. They show him how to make his way in this world by exercising self-mastery. Besides highly spiritual lessons, the Masters also teach mundane things—like catching a bus. Bit by bit they help us overcome our intimidation, which others use against us.

Full enjoyment of living comes when we become adept at managing problems in every department of our life. The ideal is to be the one who acts, not the victim of others: to be cause, not effect. Still, there are no fast rules. We can be the effect in a situation as long as we are aware of it.

But the Master often catches us napping when we ought to be awake. We spend so much time scratching for truth beneath the surface, like a hen pecking industriously in the dirt. We forget to look up and see that truth is in the making this very moment. Eventually, we put each episode of truth into perspective and see the lesson the Master was trying to teach us.

A few years ago I boarded a jumbo jet for Europe. The flight was to last many hours; therefore, I was pleased to find myself alone in a row of three seats. The plane was nearly full a few minutes before departure. I nervously watched the entrance to the cabin for late boarders. What is more discouraging than to have the last passenger on board be your seatmate and crowd you on a long flight?

I glanced around the cabin of the jumbo jet. No empty seats were in sight except the two beside me: therefore all the more a treasure. This lent visions of putting up the armrests and stretching out on the seats for a long nap. The ECK was certainly good to me on this flight.

My luck held as the flight attendant secured the cabin door, locking it. Other passengers, jammed together shoulder to shoulder, looked miserable even before take-off. Wasn't I lucky, indeed?

The plane took off, and I reclined my seat, thinking about the travel adventure awaiting me in Europe. A flight attendant interrupted my blissful reverie. "A lady has asked to sit by your window," she said. "Would you mind?" Since a part of the ECK path is giving up our little self, the ego, I answered expansively, "Of course she can!"

Feeling less expansive than I appeared, however, I wondered: If she has a seat, why take mine?

Very shortly, my new seat companion pushed and grunted her way into the window seat; I reclaimed mine in the middle. Ever ready to make the best of a bad situation, I thought: Well, why not? If I sit on the aisle, there's still an empty seat between us. But plans for my in-flight bed had certainly flown.

The little old lady appeared to be the sweetest thing— from New York, she said. "Oh, thank you for letting me sit by the window," she gushed.

"Quite all right," I said, once again magnanimous. But as I rose to take the aisle seat, her hand on my sleeve restrained me.

"By the way," she continued, a sad little droop in her voice, "my husband is still in the back of the plane." What had that to do with me?

"He has bad legs," she added, "and has to sit on the aisle so he can stretch them. Otherwise he can't even get in or out of his seat."

She paused with a particularly sorrowful look, like a sad-eyed beagle, as if not daring to trust her trembling voice to ask a further favor. But steeling herself, as she had undoubtedly done so many times before, she asked almost apologetically, "Do you suppose my husband could sit here? He'd be in the aisle seat. No trouble to you at all."

This seemingly helpless woman had likely picked up the fine art of begging on the streets of New York City. First, she got herself entrenched in a seat by *my* window. Now, hardly three minutes later, she was scheming a reunion with her feeble, damaged husband. I was too intimidated to tell her to return to the back of the plane if she wanted a seat by her husband. Also, she talked faster than I could think. So I meekly nodded my head. Yes, he could come up front. Both of us, victor and loser, knew in that moment she had outfoxed me.

Quicker than a teenager can bolt to the refrigerator for ice cream during a TV commercial, here came her spouse. He staggered up the aisle from the deep recesses of the plane. Issuing a stream of complaints, he maneuvered around until finally settling into his seat after a number of false starts.

Immediately he leaned across me in the middle seat. He wanted to talk with his wife. His expression said: What kind of a turkey sits between an old man and his wife?

From my first year in ECK, I had made a concerted effort to no longer be a victim of brassy people like this. Yet, here it had happened again. This old couple was so artful at moving into my space that I had no defense against them. I was boiling with helpless rage. But they were not done yet.

The woman sensed that something was troubling me. So she explained the situation to her husband. "This young man has offered to take your seat in the back of the plane so we can be together." In disbelief, my eyes widened to the size of saucers.

She had just done the whole routine on me. The best I could manage was a slack jaw and the aimless expression of an imbecile. In five short minutes she had given me one easy lesson in how to impose upon somebody and leave him helpless to do anything about it. As if on cue, the flight attendant appeared in the aisle. The old woman asked her to please show me to the back of the plane. And I was gone.

The flight attendant led me to absolutely the last seat in the whole plane. It was in the smoking section, by the lavatories, on the aisle. Other than that, it was fine. That was a long, long flight to Europe.

Here was the lesson: being Mr. Milquetoast is not a step toward self-mastery. I hoped that future spiritual unfoldment would prepare me for alligators like these two, who had so neatly stolen my seat from under me.

But the ECK also used this incident to polish my humility. Of all the other initiates in the ECK Office who were qualified to make this trip to Europe and speak at the ECK seminar, I was the one chosen. Now it was clear that I was the one who most needed the lesson.

This is how the spiritual hierarchy of ECK Masters operates. We are put into one raw situation after another, until we realize what the Holy Spirit is trying to give us. These were some of my experiences in the temple of the heart, as I struggled with the lessons of love, compassion, and understanding.

This was a test to see how much I would drink in one draught.
"The superior Master," the Inner Master had once said, "drinks
all of the cup of life."

7

Disappointments on the Way to ECK Mastership

Deep disappointments can lead to serious illness. I found this out in the early part of 1981, when my health turned bad in three short months. My strength and vitality were suddenly gone, and it took weeks of patient attention to the right attitude, nutrition, and exercise to begin the slow road to recovery. This is the way it began.

A year earlier, the first week of March 1980, my predecessor as the spiritual leader of ECKANKAR, Darwin Gross, had paid me a visit in the camera department at the ECKANKAR Office in Menlo Park, California. The office had moved to California in 1975. I was seated on a stool by the light table, opaqueing negatives that were to be used in making plates for the printing press. Gross leaned against the other table, made a few pleasant remarks, then asked me to accompany him into the darkroom, which was soundproof. He wanted to discuss a private matter with me.

He was my spiritual Master and held the Rod of ECK Power. I had complete faith in him because, as the agent for the SUGMAD, he often appeared to me in dreams and in Soul Travel. This was three and a half years before the unhappy events of August 1983, when his spiritual disobedience led to his later ouster from ECKANKAR.

We walked into the first of the camera rooms, and I shut the huge refrigerator door behind us. This room had once served as a cold-storage room for the building's previous owners, a pharmaceutical company. After ECKANKAR had bought the property, this room was divided into three smaller rooms, each with a special photographic function.

Then we entered a second room, which was more "inner" yet, and that door was shut, too. I wondered what was so important that he had us in such a soundproof, private room.

Amid neatly ordered trays of developer, stop bath, and fix, boxes of film and camera equipment all around us, Gross told of his plans to step aside as the Living ECK Master. Would I accept the position as his successor?

His statement, however historic, was not really a surprise to me. Paul Twitchell, by means of the Golden-tongued Wisdom of the ECK-Vidya (the Ancient Science of Prophecy), had already said that I was to be the Mahanta after the next Living ECK Master had served his term. This was back in October of 1970, at the World Wide in Las Vegas. My whole life was thereafter given over to ECK. The living truth that I had searched for so many years was the ECK, and by experience, I learned the reality of Soul Travel and the Light and Sound of God.

Besides this, and most importantly, both Peddar Zaskq (Paul Twitchell) and Dap Ren (Gross's spiritual name) had been coming to me in the Soul body for many months now, testing me in one fashion or another, to prepare me for taking the Rod of ECK Power and accepting the spiritual mantle of the Mahanta.

In answer to Gross, I said, "If that is what is to be, yes."

"Not so fast," he replied. "There's one more thing to consider. Your wife must also agree with your decision." That struck me as odd. To my mind, the spiritual leadership of ECK was a spiritual compact between the SUGMAD and the candidate for ECK Mastership. Social approval, even from one's own spouse, did not enter into the picture, to my way of thinking.

My training for Mastership was from the SUGMAD, working through ITS chief agents of the time: first Paul Twitchell, then Darwin Gross. But during their terms as spiritual leaders of ECK, the SUGMAD also gave instructions through other ECK Masters, like Rebazar Tarzs. Around Christmas in 1979, he came in the Soul body and dictated this message: "Do not make the error of trying to rule the universes, the worlds of God, by yourself—by your own dictates. It is the will of the SUGMAD, which manifests through all the spiritual hierarchy, that will assist you."

Preparations like this for the Mahantaship became a daily ritual since Paul had made his prophetic announcement to me in 1970. Rebazar was speaking to me of how the Living ECK Master goes about conducting the affairs of the worlds in a workable way. He spoke from experience, for he had been the spiritual head of the underground ECK movement in the fifteenth and sixteenth centuries. As the torchbearer of ECK, he often stood in as a spiritual guide for ECK initiates during the transition from one Living ECK Master to his heir.

For that matter, Dap Ren came in the Soul body on January 9, 1980—two weeks after Rebazar—and awarded me a sacred commission. He appeared in travel clothes, a suitcase by his feet. Before he picked it up to leave, he said, "I give you a sacred responsibility that must be fulfilled." The ECK Masters gave me this sort of inner training for nearly a decade, and each time, they left me with a greater understanding of ECK than before.

* * *

Now, here in a darkroom lab, the outer fulfillment of all the inner promises was coming to pass. The Living ECK Master had just asked whether I would be his successor. That night I told my wife of the conversation. She agreed that the will of the SUGMAD would be done, no matter what. She was given an insight into the difficulties that lay ahead of me: the health problems from helping initiates work through karma, the stress of learning to bring harmony to all levels of the ECK followers, the wearing travel-and-speaking schedule, and the loss of privacy.

There were easily a thousand good reasons to say no to the offer, because it would only bring the greatest of hardships. But the one overriding reason that left room for only a yes response was this: SUGMAD's endless love for Soul.

In the darkroom Gross had said that this change in leadership would take place at the 1980 World Wide in Los Angeles. All along, however, the ritual of the Passing of the Rod of ECK Power was being enacted for me repeatedly in the other worlds, first from one angle, then another. In March 1980, one of the Nine Silent Ones sat at a judge's bench in a crowded meeting room. Somebody asked me to step into the room, and the Silent One spoke: "Harold Klemp, please arise and approach the bench."

The roomful of people broke into applause. Hands were clapped on my shoulders in congratulations. The Silent One read an oath in a loud voice and asked me to repeat it after him. Peddar Zaskq and Dap Ren stood behind the judge's bench, watching from the wings.

Now an ECK Master approached with a gallon of water in a clear jug. "Take one swallow, only one," commanded the Silent One.

This was a test to see how much I would drink in one draught. "The superior Master," the Inner Master had once said, "drinks all of the cup of life." My eyes went wide at the size of the jug. A whole gallon? Well then, so be it; I would drink it all. And why not? This was the Living Water of Life. This was the ECK, the Holy Spirit. With the Living Water poised at my lips, but not yet wetting them, I awaited a signal from the Silent One to drink, and then I would drink it all.

This was a test to see to what degree I would fulfill my mission. Would I be one to pursue it wholeheartedly, or settle for doing it in half measures?

Or would I touch the water to my lips *before* the signal to drink was given? That would cancel the test, and for this reason: It meant a lack of self-discipline. Outwardly, it meant I would break the law of silence and talk to others about the ECK Mastership before its time. So many make the mistake of claiming the Mastership based on an inner experience alone. They have an experience of this nature on the inner planes, then assert from that one experience that others should recognize them as an ECK Master.

But breaking the bond of silence brings exactly the opposite effect: a spiritual fall. The Mahanta, the Living ECK Master is the only one who can complete the circuit between the spiritual and physical worlds. He alone can say, "This is my beloved son, the Living ECK Master of the times."

Such inner and outer preparations combine to have quite an impact on a person. The ECK Current flows into the human body in successively greater waves, but the body lags behind the spiritual changes. This lag can lead to health problems, because the vibrations of the inner and outer bodies run at greatly different speeds. It is like a driver who steps on a car accelerator to pick up speed. Then, instead of using the brakes, he drags his foot out of the car door to stop the car. But the car is far too fast and heavy for a dragging foot to halt it, and the effort tears up the sole of his shoe as well.

That is much like what happens when the Sound Current of ECK becomes greater than the individual's capacity to contain It. He ends up with a host of problems to his health, wealth, and happiness because his understanding is too puny to correctly handle the inflow of the ECK Current.

Two weeks after the first meeting in the darkroom, Gross again came into the camera room while I was preparing the presswork for Paul's *Wisdom Notes.* At the earlier discussion, Gross had said we would have a second meeting soon. Now he studied the cover of *The Wisdom Notes* book, checked the information on the copyright page, then said, "Maybe you and your wife would like to have lunch after the Creative Arts Festival." This ECK seminar was scheduled for mid-June.

Then came the ECK-Vidya to give a true perspective of the future, what to expect after the Passing of the Rod of ECK Power. I had awakened one night with a loud shout, "Paul!"

The reason for the cry was this: On the inner planes I had become the new Living ECK Master, and former students of Twitchell and Gross were causing problems. They had fallen into the self-deception of personality worship because they were ignorant about the true nature of the Mahanta. One of the groups formed around the personality of Paul Twitchell; they called themselves "Paul's Followers." The other group was Gross's supporters.

Neither body could accept me as the newest manifestation of the ECK. They chose the dead past over the dynamic present, and their excuse was that my spiritual caliber was less than that of the previous two Masters. This is a well-worn response known to every Living ECK Master, since people's patterns of behavior have changed but little through the centuries.

The Gross faction was the stronger of the two. During the inner experience that led to my outcry, members of that group had tried to waylay me in a dark maze of alleys. But the strength of the Mahanta, the everlasting ECK, came upon me in a tremendous wave to confound and defeat the attackers.

When I called Paul's name, it had nothing to do with his personality. It was a cry to the primal Mahanta—there is none other—for help. This was the same supreme consciousness that I now realize had manifested in Paul during the current age of ECK. To call upon Its might, I had shouted, "Paul!" That was the linkup.

Now I walked within the safety of the power and love of the Mahanta. The false ECKists had hidden in walls and alleys in order to ambush me. I tore down their hiding places to the last cornerstone. With no place left to hide, all those who were selfish and lusted for power were swept away into darkness. The new ECKists who came into ECKANKAR were good people, builders. They, and those who had remained loyal to the principle of the Mahanta, were eager to serve as Co-workers for the SUGMAD.

This prophetic glimpse of the future came on March 17, 1980—a year and a half before the mantle of ECK Mastership was placed upon my shoulders.

It was a solitary burden to carry all this knowledge of the future and not be able to tell anyone about it. One must keep in mind that the ECK Mastership is a result of a union of inner and outer experience. The final bridge to Mastership is crossed when the current Living ECK Master, on the physical plane, names his own successor.

Right in the middle of the maelstrom surrounding the final stages of training for ECK Mastership came the publishing of my first book, *The Wind of Change*. It had been almost two years in the writing, and every possible obstacle that one could imagine had come up to prevent its publication. But now it was finally printed.

The printer sent five advance copies of the finished book to the ECK Office. They arrived at noon, and by one o'clock everything that could go wrong in the printing department, did. To begin with, a pressman came to me for an approval of a press sheet. A visual check, which is all this job required, was not good enough for him that day. He insisted upon a full rule-up, a time-consuming annoyance. I was up to my ears in camera work, and there was no time for petty delays like that—nevertheless it was quicker to give him a rule-up than to waste even more time in an argument.

Then my wife called and added another worry. Our daughter, who was seven, was sick at school. My wife was leaving work to take her home. After her phone call, I went into the darkroom and accidentally ruined a negative by putting a kink in it. That meant reshooting it. Next, the graphics department sent me a photo that was completely unfit for printing, so I set up the airbrush and lost another hour of precious production time.

All were minor irritations, but the book's publication did release a flood of spiritual currents that set new problems on top of those that already weighed on me, such as the very real possibility of accepting the Rod of ECK Power in six months' time.

The book's completion also saw an increase in the flow of ECK in our home. The morning after the advance copies had come to the office, my daughter awoke in time for breakfast, recovered from her unexplained illness of the day before. It was Saturday morning, a day of rest and play. As she walked into the living room, she was surprised to see a bright orange-red light there. In addition, a golden yellow spot shone on the ceiling, and a yellow ray of light beamed from it down to the floor. Out of curiosity she stepped into the golden light and immediately threw up twice. The weekend was off to a running start. The lights in the living room were of the ECK, but their vibratory rates were greater than those of our family unit. This accounted for my daughter's reaction when she stood in the beam of yellow light. But we soon grew accustomed to the spiritual changes brought by *The Wind of Change,* and home life returned to normal.

In April, my expectations for ECK Mastership were boosted to new heights when I made a Soul Travel journey to a secret monastery in the spiritual city of Agam Des, which is hidden in the remote Himalayas. Dap Ren had called for a number of Higher Initiates to come there in the Soul form. He said that the ECK leaders had to fit in with the dress of their communities, to be accepted by the people at home. This was in the way of small talk while the last of the stragglers arrived for the meeting.

When everybody was present, we all changed into new clothing provided for the occasion. The group was then led to what looked like an ordinary building set against the base of a mountain. A secret passageway in the back of the building led to a monastery hidden in the mountain. Not even the city's own people, tight-lipped and trustworthy as they were, guessed that a school of wisdom was hidden in their community.

While the rest of the group was given leadership training, Yaubl Sacabi—guardian of the Shariyat-Ki-Sugmad in Agam Des—took me on a tour of the monastery. He later turned me over to a white-haired ECK Master who lived and worked in the monastery's library. On the way to the library, the ECK Master showed me how skilled monks had sealed off the passageway into the monastery after our group's arrival. These precautions were to keep intact the secret of the monastery's location.

"This secrecy is needed to safeguard the Shariyat," he

explained. But he did not take me into the room where the holy book of ECK was kept.

The summer passed. Every little while, it seemed, I was given a dry run on the inner planes to play the role of the new Living ECK Master. Each episode was different, and each was to shore up another side of my spiritual development.

But the lessons on the outer also left their mark in my consciousness. True unfoldment stirs up both inner and outer experiences and blends them into a unified whole. For example, gossips are not clear channels for ECK. The ECK puts such people through the mill until this deadly habit is ground up and blown away. Even a little tale-bearing hurts the individual. Gossip is a child of anger, one of the five destructive actions of the mind, and it shuts off a part of the Sound and Light. This, in turn, hinders one in his contributions of service to God.

ECK taught me the folly of gossip by a good blow to my wallet. My first wife and I lived in the San Francisco area during the summer of 1980. This one weekend she had an invitation to speak at an ECK Regional Seminar in Phoenix, Arizona, and I was driving her to the airport. On the Bayshore Freeway we got into a conversation about another person's private life. An alarm bell finally went off inside me, and I asked, ''Do you suppose we're gossiping?'' But only other people gossip, so we agreed that our discussion was simple fact—not gossip, certainly. We kept on talking.

All during this time, morning rush-hour traffic was moving around us very fast in the four lanes of traffic. I kept a close watch in the mirror and over my shoulder during lane changes.

A terrible screeching and bumping noise suddenly shattered the tranquility in our car. Instinctively I clasped the steering wheel in an iron grip, in case a tire had blown out and the car pulled into another lane. Then, in the rearview mirror, I saw a muffler bouncing wildly on the road, cars swerving to avoid it.

"Say," I said, wild-eyed, "somebody lost his muffler back there. I think I drove right over it!"

Our little Japanese car did indeed have a strange sound to it now. When we left home, it had hummed like an efficient and grandmotherly sewing machine. Now it produced a deep sound like thunder. It rumbled like a semi-trailer hauling a load of logs through a high pass in the Rocky Mountains.

As an afterthought, I asked, "You don't suppose it was ours, do you?"

In fact it was, as an inspection under the car at the airport proved. The lesson in the Golden-tongued Wisdom was so obvious it was impossible to miss: "Muffle your opinions about others."

Of course, once the ECK sets a lesson into motion, it is too late to promise to be good and then expect a new muffler to appear out of thin air, invisible hands fastening it under the car again. There is always more to the original experience—the conclusion. And the conclusion has a price tacked onto it that gives a pretty fair estimate of the gravity of the offense. The price of this lesson, according to the bill from the repair shop: $87.17.

But there was also an up side to my spiritual progress. On May 23, in the afternoon, the Living ECK Master asked me into his office. This turned out to be the holy occasion of my Seventh Initiation. An initiate never speaks of the ritual unless at the risk of losing all he has gained spiritually. The initiation began a time of immense unfoldment that eclipsed anything up until then. It was a turning point, and things sped up in my life just as he had said they would during the initiation.

The Creative Arts Festival in mid-June came and went without further word from the Living ECK Master about having lunch with my wife and me. But at the seminar on June 14, 1980, Dap Ren did give me the Eighth Initiation on the inner planes.

"The Initiate of the Eighth Circle never complains despite the most difficult circumstances," said Dap Ren. "He is filled with the Light and Love of the Supreme One at all times." He added that all initiations beyond the Eighth are given on the invisible planes alone.

Seven and a half months later, on January 27, 1981, I got the outer initiation in San Francisco.

A natural question one might ask about the ECK Initiations is this: "If Paul Twitchell had God-Realization in 1957, why did the ECK Master Shamus-i-Tabriz suggest that Paul was not omniscient?" Isn't a God-Realized person supposed to know all things?

After Paul's journey with Rebazar Tarzs to the Anami (God), Shamus said of Paul in *The Tiger's Fang:* "Then he should know all things, but I see by the light around him there are many things yet that he needs to know before being accepted into the ancient order of the Bourchakoun!" But Shamus answered his own question in the next breath: "No man, nor Soul, ever reaches the fulfillment of the quest for God. One goes on and on and on throughout all eternity, deeper into perfection and deeper into God."

Paul did have the experience of God Consciousness in 1957, but it took eight full years before he was ready for the mantle of the Mahanta in 1965. Even then he did not know all things, as the spiritually naive would like to think he did.

In my case, I had this experience of God in 1970. But then followed eleven years of the most difficult and exacting training as I made my way through the outer and inner initiations. It took that long to consolidate and "set" each higher level of initiation. The initiation of God-Realization is such that all unworthiness is torn out of one. All the strength that the individual has ever gathered over the centuries to bring him to this high plateau is without meaning, for the majesty of the SUGMAD is beyond anything in ITS creation.

The summer rolled on by, and my spiritual experiences were of the Sound and Light of God, Rebazar Tarzs, Peddar Zaskq, Dap Ren, and other ECK Masters, but there was no further word in the outer world from the Living ECK Master on a plan to pass the Rod of ECK Power at the World Wide Seminar in Los Angeles on October 22.

There was one exception to the silence. In September, a small group of Higher Initiates were invited to be at Sedona, Arizona, for the dedication of the ECK Spiritual Center. But that turned into a disappointment, too. The ceremony was to take place the weekend before the seminar, but a cancellation letter came from the ECK Office a few days before the dedication. The postponement was the ECK speaking through the Golden-tongued Wisdom that the Rod of ECK Power would also see a delay, but I did not want to think so.

By then I had already made arrangements for vacation time, to drive down to Arizona with my wife and daughter. Even though the dedication of the ECK Spiritual Center was called off, we decided to go ahead with the trip on our own, then drive on to the seminar in Los Angeles. The only noteworthy part of the trip is the food poisoning I got from spoiled peanut butter, which left me moaning all night long, while my family slept in peace, exhausted from the hot drive in the desert.

The effects of the food poisoning let up by morning, but

I was left very weak. My wife shared the driving, and we managed to get to the hotel in Los Angeles without further incident.

Uncertain of what to expect at the seminar, and not having heard any word from the Living ECK Master, I was afraid to attend his talks. Would he just announce my appointment out of the blue? I was not in the best condition to accept the Rod of ECK Power, so I sat far back in the auditorium, tired and weak from the bad peanut butter.

At one point in his talk, Gross said that whoever was next in line for the ECK Mastership had failed the test. What a blow! Taking into account the inner and outer events of the past year, I naturally took this to mean me. A while later, however, I was to learn that several other candidates had been tested. The Master-in-training who failed the final tests could have been any one of us; indeed, all of us, since no one became the new Living ECK Master.

Hearing of the unknown candidate's failure, I threw up my hands in despair. What more could the SUGMAD want? Hadn't I given up everything in my heart and being so that ITS divine love could fill me at will? What more could one do?

The eight-hour drive home was a ride of lonely frustration. "Don't worry," my wife said, trying to console me, "You can always be an ECK Master, even if you can't be the Living ECK Master."

"That's not what Paul told me," I said, reminding her of Paul's prophecy in 1970. "What he told me is right, or my direction in ECK has been wrong for ten years."

From then on the unfulfilled promise of Mastership haunted me every waking and sleeping moment. I did not fall into a state of despair, but became even more determined than ever to realize my goal of God-Realization. Everything I did was in the name of the SUGMAD, and if any element of the little self remained in me, I had no heart left to feed its whims. My heart ached for the love of God, for without that, life was without meaning.

More than once my wife tried in vain to cheer me up by saying that it is a blessing to become an ECK Master; why not set my sights on that? It certainly is a blessing to become an ECK Master, but that was not the fullness of my vision. Finally, I refused to discuss anything at all about my inner life. Until then we had often shared our inner experiences, but anything that was even a slight detraction from my ultimate goal might prove to be the straw that would keep me from Oneness with the ECK. From then on I no longer spoke about my inner experiences, and at the time, this strained our marriage badly.

Another aftermath of the World Wide Seminar was that a number of Higher Initiates left ECKANKAR in a huff. Rumors had been afoot at the seminar that a group of dissenters had chosen a spokesman to challenge Gross's right to Mastership. This challenge was to be made from the audience during one of his talks, but the plan for such a radical move fell through when the spokesman for the group thought better of the idea and no one else had the nerve to do it for him.

The feelings of the dissenting group then split two ways. The hotheads still wanted a face-to-face confrontation with Gross during his talk, but the cooler heads pointed to the Shariyat, which says that a Living ECK Master names his own successor. Until this change in succession came about in a natural way, the ECK still had more lessons in store for the initiates under the leadership of Gross. The second group rightly argued that the naming of a new Master is under the supervision of the spiritual hierarchy and was not subject to a democratic vote.

In early December 1980, I had an experience on the inner planes where several of these rebels had nevertheless continued their fight to unseat Gross as the spiritual leader of ECK. They went to an ECK reading room and put big sheets of paper into books that stood up like signs. A few read: "Darwin is not the Master," "No one dare stand between God and man," and other like phrases.

I simply took the cards out of the books and said, "Nobody needs that!" So ended the problem.

In the meantime Peddar Zaskq continued my spiritual training by speeding up my comprehension of the ECK-Vidya. The discipline was to find the key to greater awareness. He impressed upon me an image of a structural formation with a myriad of details.

"What do you see?" he asked.

Patiently I began to convert the subtle mental symbol into descriptive words, because one must develop the faculty of clear vision when learning to express what he sees of the ECK-Vidya. What I saw in the future was not to my liking at all, so I left it out of my private journal, hoping that I had read the future wrong.

The future that was revealed had caught me entirely off guard. It was not at all concerned with the Rod of ECK Power, even though the shock of having been passed over for ECK Mastership still had me in anguish two months later. Instead, the future showed a serious health problem for my older brother. This seemed impossible, so I tried to dismiss the bleak picture from my mind. He was in the best of health, had a loving wife and a beautiful family. He loved his work as a pilot.

The ECK-Vidya must be wrong. It wasn't possible that a serious illness could threaten my brother's life.

The closeness between my older brother and me had been left somewhat in tatters since 1967, when I had come into ECKANKAR. My interests had gone toward Self- and God-Realization, while he tended toward the psychic studies. For a while he got caught up in automatic handwriting. He wrote several long letters to me in Japan, where I was in the Air Force, telling of all the predictions this wonderful ability lent him. My knowledge of ECK was that of a novice, but I had the sense to see that automatic handwriting left an individual under the control of an untried, outer influence. I warned him of the danger of an evil spirit possessing him, if he kept playing around with this psychic game.

His letters became an embarrassment. Each one showed that he had put more and more trust in this invisible entity that claimed to hold the future in his omniscient powers. But the psychic entity went too far once, and this ended my brother's flirtation with forces from the other worlds that he was ill prepared to handle.

One day the entity who controlled his pen wrote a prophecy with dire consequences for the family. The note said that his wife's brother, a soldier in Vietnam, would be killed in action. The government would notify the family about his death on a certain day, at two o'clock in the afternoon. My brother debated whether he should risk asking his supervisor for a day off on some pretext, so he could be there to comfort his wife at the loss of her brother.

I could hardly wait to read the next letter after the deadline given in the automatic handwriting. Did his brother-in-law really die in battle? Did the official notice come at two o'clock in the afternoon? I tore the letter open and read what really happened. It was quite different from what my brother had expected.

On the appointed day he "just happened" to be home. His wife wondered why he had taken off work and then wasted the day by puttering in his home office, instead of making a special day of it. My brother steeled himself as the minute hand crept closer to the hour. Finally—two o'clock! But the phone and the doorbell both remained silent. Then he began to calculate the difference in time zones between the Midwest and Vietnam, thinking that perhaps he was eleven hours off his estimate. But still no word from the government about the fate of his wife's brother.

In fact, after a few days, it was obvious that the entity responsible for the automatic handwriting had made a glaring error. The young soldier was in good health and later came home from the war unscathed.

My brother asked why the psychic entity had let him make such a fool of himself. The entity replied that conditions had changed since it made the prediction, but wasn't my brother glad that his brother-in-law was safe? Even my brother could see how the psychic forces were playing with him, and soon after that he gave up automatic handwriting for good.

My brother was an enthusiastic man who threw himself completely into every project he began. That is the quality that had made him an excellent air traffic controller at one of the most active military airfields in the United States at the time—Chanute Air Force Base in Illinois. He was stationed there during the Cuban Missile Crisis in 1962, when the sky was full of fighters, bombers, and transports to curb the Russian threat.

He was a short man, a mere quarter of an inch shy of the minimum height requirements for Air Force pilots. When he failed the medical exam because of this fraction of an inch, his flying career suffered a setback. He missed out on hundreds of hours of flying time in military planes, and instead spent his time in a control tower. Off duty he flew in the aero club, but this did not make up for all the flight time he would have accrued as a full-time pilot.

Nevertheless it was enough of a flying background to get him a position with a feeder airline soon after he left the Air Force in the mid-1960s. But he never made the jump from propeller-driven planes to pure jets, which was his dream.

Outer confirmation of his ill health came in a phone call from my mother at seven o'clock on a Sunday morning, in the middle of January 1981. She said that doctors had found malignant growths in him.

Later in the day I called him and found his attitude both positive and cheerful. He had received a copy of *The Wind of Change* in the mail, and "A Cow Tale" struck him as particularly funny. It is the chapter where Dad climbed sheepishly out of the ditch after driving the tractor into it while chasing a cow.

Five days after that we talked again. The doctors now said that the cancer had spread throughout his lymph glands and was further advanced than an early diagnosis had shown. He was scheduled for chemotherapy and radium treatments, and the whole idea of the seriousness of his illness was hard for him to accept, especially since it had not yet begun to tax his strength.

In passing, I mentioned that he could ask for a spiritual healing from the ECK, besides his regular medical treatment, but that idea did not appeal to him. This was understandable, because he was a Lutheran. The ways of ECK were not a part of his understanding.

My brother's illness made a dramatic change in my own attitude in ECK. Until then I was like so many other initiates, trying to lead the "detached" life that would win me God's grace sooner. The only problem is, like them, I misinterpreted "detached" to mean "an absolute separation from all the good things in life." Like so many other ECKists, I was an outsider looking down at the world from a lofty pinnacle. But it was a cold and lonesome place.

"Detachment" really means to have an objective viewpoint of life. This is necessary for spiritual survival. But the kind of exclusion from the human race that I drew from the meaning of "detachment" was actually a warping of the emotions. ECKists are not alone in falling into austere practices in the mistaken belief that this will make them more worthy in the sight of God.

The old Christian idea that the world is an evil place that must be shunned is a concept that is just as peculiar.

Would God have invested so much time and patience in this earthly slum unless it were for some purpose? Just because theologians cannot agree on a master plan for earth's creation does not mean that God did not have one. Or does it?

In any case, this family crisis forced me to take a long, hard look at the meaning of detachment. Was it really fear of living that caused me to desire a detached life? If I felt compassion for my brother, would that open my inner bodies for taking on his karma? After all, he made the karma that produced this sickness. Why should I take a chance and get it, too?

What person in his right mind would involve himself in something as deadly as cancer?

The real issue turned out to be not detachment at all, but surrender. Only later did I again read the beautiful chapter on love in *Stranger by the River*, "No Greater Love." Rebazar Tarzs, the Tibetan ECK Master, and the seeker were in an old graveyard on a hot day in April. On one of the gravestones was this inscription: "No Greater Love Hath Man Than To Lay Down His Life For Another." The seeker explained that the stone marked the grave of a low-caste Hindu who had given his life to save a white child from drowning in the river.

Rebazar said, "It is true that when man gives his life for another that he will be saved. That Soul touched the unseen power which we call the sea of life. By doing so he gained God's mercy and grace for himself!"

The moment that we give up all thoughts for our own well-being is the moment that we are closest to God.

Everyone in the family pulled together to give my brother support and also information on other methods of healing. My wife's uncle had won two rounds in his bout with cancer. He had gone to a clinic in Mexico, and the doctors there put him on a strict diet and gave him a medicine not available in the United States.

My sister hoped to raise several thousand dollars for

medical costs, but my brother declined her offer. His insurance would cover the cost of the treatments.

But what could I offer? It certainly was not money. I was an employee at the ECK Office, working at a smaller salary than at my previous employer. My wife also worked in the ECK Office, and her salary was even less than mine. And there was our daughter, whose day-care tuition and other expenses for food and clothing were sometimes breathtaking. That is because she was a fast-growing eight-year-old, who outgrew her clothes faster than we could buy her new ones.

The best I could offer was to call my brother and listen to him talk. I would have done anything to help him win his battle with death, even to the point of giving up my own life.

And by calling him on the phone every week, I came close to doing just that. My willingness to help him was in effect what opened me as an "attached" vehicle for the ECK. The risk was taking on his karma, and perhaps, his illness.

During our phone conversations I saw a wonderful thing: My brother was again becoming the warm, open individual he had been before enlisting in the Air Force after high school graduation. He had been too busy to write many letters, and the ones that came were clearly in the line of social duty. After military service, he got a job at a local airport, a half hour from home; but with his work hours and social life he hardly ever came to see us on the farm. He had changed from a young idealist, with high dreams for the future, to a busy pilot who was too caught up in a rush to visit his family.

The changes in him had left me a little sad. His once beautiful, warm nature was swallowed up by the crisp business world of aviation.

But his illness mellowed him back to the seventeen-year-old brother I remembered. He talked of the walks he and his wife now took at sunset, trying to comfort each other as he underwent the ordeal of chemotherapy. He began to spend more time with his oldest son, who was about to become a teenager. He talked of when he was plowing the fields at the tender age of six, and how the jarring of the tractor seat, which had no shock absorber, had damaged his spine. One day the pain was so great that he crawled home on hands and knees, because he could not walk. Weed-killers and fertilizers were another topic of conversation. He was determined to learn what had caused his cancer; he would be a guinea pig for the doctors. Maybe, through his sacrifice, they would find a cure to help others.

In looking back, my life had been rocked to its core in a matter of three months. First, my dreams for ECK Mastership seemed hopelessly dashed. Right after that, my brother was diagnosed as a terminally ill patient. What else could go wrong in my worlds of ECK?

I was soon to find out.

Cannonballs, made up to look like softballs, tore up the field around me as I crouched in quiet desperation behind my glove, trying to be as small a target as possible.

8

A Long, Hard Haul

My health was good on January 11, 1981, the day my mother called to tell me of my brother's cancer. But in three months' time my health would take a sharp turn for the worse.

The ECK Mastership again seemed a far-off dream; it was a spiritual calamity to have been passed over for the Rod of ECK Power in October 1980. One of these shocks was about all I could handle at once, but with two of them back-to-back, it stood to reason there might be a backlash. The ECK Mastership, as a goal for achievement, became of secondary importance after the news of my brother's illness. Still, I wanted more deeply than ever to be a better and clearer channel for ECK.

By the end of January, a subtle lethargy had begun to steal over me. This first became apparent after my eight-year-old daughter and I had finished a picture in her coloring book and I tried to get up from the floor. ''Put the book away and get ready for bed,'' I said, warding off her pleas to stay up a little longer.

There was a difference in how we each got up from the floor: She sprang up as if it were morning, while I had to gather all my determination to pull myself up. I regarded this sluggishness as an early sign of aging and tried to put it from my mind.

In the coming month I could not help but notice my energy level had taken a sharp drop. I was perplexed about this change but did not tie it in with my concern for my brother.

Our phone conversations—between him in Wisconsin and me in California—went on weekly. At first it was hard to accept the fact of his cancer, but maybe my "attached" regard for his well-being had taken a wrong turn. It was one thing to care about somebody's welfare, but quite another to harbor sentiments that clashed with his choice of treatment.

He chose chemotherapy in his battle against cancer, but I asked him to also consider treatment in the Mexican clinic that had helped my wife's uncle. My opinion, at best, was a decision at arm's length, but for him it was a matter of life or death. After all, his life was at stake. If I had given wholehearted support to his decision, it would have shown a true, detached viewpoint.

"Cease to cherish opinions" is a well-known saying in ECK. Opinions create more trouble than people can imagine. Like gossip, they fly back to strike the sender. The ECK-Vidya warned me to stop giving my brother any further advice about the Mexican clinic—because he did not want it—but I missed the warning that came during the following experience on the inner planes.

On the Astral Plane, I came upon a group of young men tossing a football. The ball bounced loose and rolled toward me. Instinctively, I scooped it up and threw an underhand spiral pass to the nearest player, but the football never reached him. A peculiar thing happened as the football flew toward him: its flight slowed, then stopped in midair. The football was caught in a whirling vortex of an energy field just beyond the fingertips of the receiver. Then the ball exploded free from the vortex and hurled back at me with tremendous speed. I ducked to the ground as the projectile shot by, inches from my head.

This experience spoke of karma. Any underhanded thought, word, or action returns straight to its sender. But the broad implications of this inner counsel had eluded me. Its warning went beyond the evils of gossip, a lesson I had learned earlier when the muffler fell off my car. The ECK was here showing the danger of butting into another person's life under the guise of caring.

Meddling is an underhanded act, and without knowing it, I had taken on some of my brother's karma.

My body had always been in good condition. It quickly rebounded from any abuse that I had put it to during my youth, while still ignorant of the laws of health. I had fed it with cases of soft drinks, cartons full of ice cream, cookies, pies, and cakes. Pizza—dripping with melted cheese (a farmer's delight!), tomato sauce, and spicy pepperoni—was certainly a gift from heaven. And to show appreciation for such a boon, I always ate the whole thing.

The dentist was in my mouth second only to sweets, but who really wants to think there is a connection between the pleasure of sweets and the pain of decay? Anyway, cavities were accepted as a normal misfortune of life. A surgical operation or the Asian flu were signs of real sickness, but certainly not cavities. Life, for the most part, was a matter of good or bad luck, especially when it concerned the onset of pain from sweets.

Therefore, to me, cavities did not belong under the heading of health. Health meant other things: the ability to run when I felt like it, without pain in the joints. It meant walking the home streets of Mountain View, California, for hours—without tiredness. It also meant the capacity to work with speed and efficiency in ECKANKAR's camera department. A healthy body would do that, but it was distressing to find it was no longer so. For one thing, my step had slowed. This slowing took place over a few weeks' time. The sharp contrast between my "before" and "after" energy left no doubt that my body was undergoing rapid changes for the worse.

By the end of February 1981, the Inner Master was sending signals of an impending crisis in my health that might end in death. My health had become a question of survival. In the experience that follows, I was reminded to chant HU, to call up every possible survival technique to prolong my stay in the body. When one sings HU, a special name for God, he agrees to let Spirit do what is best for him. The chant does not guarantee a healing, but it does arrange for the conditions that are best for spiritual unfoldment.

On the inner planes, then, night had fallen as I picked my way along a narrow mountain ridge. The path came to an especially precarious ledge, and I crept carefully along it in the dark. My fingers clutched at the scrubby bushes that clung to the shallow topsoil on the inside of the rocky trail.

Then my stomach did a flip as a slight movement warned of the earth sliding toward the edge of the precipice. There was no time to scramble to safe ground. The avalanche carried along everything in its path. The bush that I clung to in desperation slid over the ledge, and I with it—into the black abyss of eternity.

I fell through a great space and shut my eyes against the inevitable crash of flesh and bone at the bottom of the immeasurable gulf. With a last effort, however, I cleared my mind, searching for help in this final moment of existence. The word HU came to my lips, and I sang it softly in the rushing wind.

A second later, it seemed, I was awake at the bottom. The blackness was gone and the landscape was bathed in a searing white light that left no shadows. And there stood the Inner Master, who walked thoughtfully among the rocks that were strewn with clothing and bits of flesh.

"Come, let's go!" he said.

I never looked back at my empty shell, which lay crumpled on the rocky ground like a broken doll. As Soul, the Eternal, it was a simple matter to step from it into a higher and finer body on another, greater plane of existence. This was in one of the heavens of God.

The dream meant that circumstances would take me over the edge of life. My old spiritual self would see death, but like the phoenix, I would arise to a grander life. A whole new world lay ahead, awaiting discovery. The secret of survival during this ordeal would be in the HU chant, which must be my companion in every moment of the most dire trouble. In HU lay hope. In it was the promise of a more abundant life, which would arise from the ruins of my old temple. This experience faced me with the harsh reality of the future—that my life was in jeopardy. But the censor was successful in shielding me from the warning, for I did not understand the experience upon awakening.

When I reflected upon it later, it was curious how much the same I felt after the accident as before it. My identity and beingness did not depend upon any particular body that chanced to cover me. When the Inner Master and I had walked off to explore the mysteries of this bright new world of ECK, there was no regret in leaving the empty shell behind; it was as useless as a worn-out shoe.

My brother's treatment was a painful ordeal. Without belaboring the details, which he recounted by phone, the treatments always left him very ill for several days. And during the course of his treatment, I grew steadily weaker.

The weakness showed when I drove our car, which was not equipped with power steering. Nevertheless, it was a small foreign car and required only a light hand for steering; but lately it had seemed to handle more like a truck. One Saturday I even checked the air pressure in the tires, thinking that the hard steering was due to underinflated tires. By and by it dawned on me that the fault lay in my strength. Finally awakened to the seriousness of the problem, I began to compare the condition of my body with that of others my age. These observations made me uneasy.

Another thing that changed was my formerly fast walk. Walking was always a favorite pastime: it let me sift the chaff from my thoughts. Walking was also a means of transportation. Ours was a one-car family, and after my first wife left the ECK Office, she used the car to commute to her new job. This worked well because the bus and train service was good over the nine miles from home to Menlo Park, site of the ECK Office. But it still meant a mile or two of walking every day to make connections, and this required a fast walk.

My gait had always been fast and smooth, but lately it was jerky. The leg muscles tired easily and tightened overnight. Each day it became harder to get to the train or bus stop for the first segment of the commute. This deterioration in my ability to walk was another clue that the human machine was breaking down.

The last thing to draw my attention was the condition of the backs of my hands. In the past weeks, light wrinkles had begun to etch their fine lines there, and then the fine lines became deep grooves. The pattern they made was like the spider webs of broken safety glass. The wrinkles got so bad that even a clenched fist would not make them disappear. Whose body was this anyway?

Observation also showed that the hands of other people my age were in better shape than mine: even those of people thirty years older. I began to walk with my hands stuck deep in my pockets. The skin damage was not due to photographic or printing chemicals, because I always wore rubber gloves while handling them.

Although I kept a sharp eye on my health, my attention was also on the Higher Initiates who had quit ECKANKAR after the 1980 World Wide Seminar. Most were once friends, and now they strutted like peacocks, thinking they had beaten the law of karma. Nothing bad had happened to them since they left ECKANKAR, so maybe the warnings in *The Shariyat-Ki-Sugmad,* the Bible of ECK, were off target.

The *Shariyat,* Book Two, states: "Those who are believers in name only of the ECK (expecting It to take care of them), and are vain, haughty, and do not take the word of the Living ECK Master seriously, will always have to bear the burden of their troubles."

However, since their lives after leaving ECK were little changed from before, they took it as proof that their accusations about Gross were right: namely, he was a false Master. If he were the true one, would the ECK not have punished them for their criticism of him?

Be that as it may, the lords of karma never hurry justice. As long as those individuals stay within their present states of consciousness, their lives will go on as before. But if they ever think about continuing toward God-Realization, then the old debts created by their betrayal of the Master are recalled for payment. That is when they enter the school of hard knocks. Typically, since their blind spot is vanity, they will not be able to understand that the cause for all their trouble is themselves.

The rebels of 1980 may have been right in their gauging of Gross at that early date, but they forgot that he still held the Rod of ECK Power. He remained the agent of the SUGMAD until October 22, 1981. By 1983, however, events caught up with him; his spiritual insubordination led to his removal from the Order of Vairagi Adepts.

The undoing of this group which leveled its criticism at Gross was impatience—a near cousin of anger. They did not see that the ECK was in charge all along, taking care of the situation in Its own way. Impatience and vanity caused these people to react to Gross three years too soon. They were caught up in the swell of social justice and had no idea of the spiritual factors that hung in the balance.

* * *

Everything in my life was up in the air: my health was worse, leading initiates had deserted ECKANKAR and were raising doubts in others about ECK, and there was still no inner or outer word of whether I was in the running to be the new Living ECK Master. In a practical sense, I kept out of sight in the office to avoid attention, and put all my energy into the camera work. Yet sometimes the slipshod office procedures forced me to raise a voice of protest. The editors were too often careless in checking articles in the early stages of production and then insisted on major changes at the press, a costly and time-consuming practice.

Sometimes their revisions seemed petty, an attempt to impress the production crew with their importance. This did not go over well at all. Pressmen have little patience with those in printing or publishing who do not have a command of their own field and try to bluff their way. A press is unforgiving of a pressman: it responds to know-how, not to bluster. A pressman may be just as unforgiving as his machine, because they share the same dislikes. A printer's contempt lodges with an editor as easily as with the newest apprentice in the bindery.

Once, in jest, I said to a pressman that it is a good habit to leave one glaring error for an editor when preparing a job for press. When the editor caught the mistake, he felt as if he had made his contribution for the day. That relieved him of the urge to make minor last-minute changes to the text.

This poor attempt at humor got back to the general manager, who had no sense of humor whatsoever. News of my joke had come to him by way of the office grapevine, which seems to have a special operator at the switchboard to speed along such information by giving it a priority clearance. He demanded to know if I were sabotaging our printing jobs. Of course, this was nonsense. He finally accepted my word that an ECK initiate could only do everything to the best of his ability, in the name of the SUGMAD. With a final bluster of authority, he sent me from his office.

A humbler and wiser person, I beat a retreat to the darkroom and pulled the door shut, losing myself in honest camera duties. Hereafter, for all I cared, those editors could take the rest of the Kali Yuga learning their craft.

It was hard, nonetheless, to stand aside and watch the bumblings of these self-taught editors. My training as a proofreader in a large printing house had let me study the ways of real editors. The editorial and proofing procedures in the ECK Office at that time were both clumsy and ineffective. As cameraman, I routinely caught errors missed by the editors and proofreaders. After the scolding from the manager, however, I resolved to quit my sideline of proofing, and this then forced an upgrade to the proofing system.

The experience showed the folly of making jokes around vain people. Even more, it served as a reminder for the merits of the law of silence.

Meanwhile, to keep the ECK channel inside me open, I enlarged my Sunday morning hobby of putting ECK posters on public bulletin boards. The drive lasted three hours on a well-planned route. Sunday morning was ideal for postering because of light traffic. Most people were in church or slept in, and it was possible to cover a large territory in a short time.

I kept a careful tally of the number of reply cards taken from posters during the previous week. Each poster held five cards, and only on rare occasions were all reply cards taken from the pocket of the poster. Still, the weekly tally showed a consistent average of about twenty-five inquiries. That meant a hundred per month, and twelve hundred a year. It made me wonder what a concerted effort like this in all parts of the world would do to bring the ECK message to people hungry for truth.

My posters went in Laundromats (where people had time to think while waiting for their wash), shopping malls, and supermarkets. But as my illness became worse, the ECK (through the ECK Masters) directed me to community hospitals, rest homes, and clinics. Only later did this link between the inner and outer worlds become apparent: the sicker I got, the more the ECK had me put up posters or drop off ECK books and literature at hospitals—where the sick came for treatment.

The ECK Masters were also busy in the meantime, doing all in their power to cure my physical body from the inner planes. Therefore, in the outer world, they directed me to hospitals.

This was in accordance with the principle "As above, so below." As they gave these inner healings, I had to be in the vicinity of healing centers in order to complete the spiritual circuit. That is how it was. A spiritual interaction of this nature demonstrates the law of economy. The ECK employs Its channels at the place of need, without regard to age, health, location, or any other limitations. It uses every circumstance to reach people with the Light and Sound.

The poster route was a small way to return love to the ECK, a way to say thank you for the gift of consciousness. In looking back, it is noteworthy to see how the ECK steered me away from hospitals after my health showed signs of improvement.

The last Sunday in March 1981, the ECKANKAR Office was to sponsor a leadership training at Stanford University. This meeting was for over three hundred ECK leaders from northern California. On the previous Friday, one of

162

the trainers asked me to give a five-minute talk on the art of postering.

On Sunday morning, the talk on postering was not even on the program. No one had bothered to tell me of the change in plans. What the meeting did show, however, was that the ECK Office was giving lip service to the idea of field leadership. The leaders were being treated like children. They could make a few local decisions, but nothing of consequence. The ECK Office never got around to drawing up a comprehensive plan for the delegation of field duties.

Helen Baird, one of the trainers, saw through this charade. The part of the training, which she was to help lead, said: "The ECK leaders in the field are ECKANKAR, not the ECK Office." Helen noted that if this were true, why did the trainers talk so much and the "leaders" so little?

There was little unity in the group. At first nobody seemed able to say or offer anything of value, including the trainers. No one, that is, except Helen. She woke up the people in the room, challenging them with questions: "The young man asked you, 'What is ECKANKAR?' You gave him a lot of answers in general, but nobody ever answered that question."

She also raised the issue of leaders who talk but do not listen. The trainers today had set a bad example by doing most of the talking. What would the audience learn from their example? Would they, in turn, hog the floor during meetings in the ECK Center at home? A long silence followed. To me, it seemed a nearly hopeless job to someday pull together all the loose strands of leadership in ECK and weave them into a single strong bond of unity.

Yet the Order of Vairagi Adepts carries out its work through a code of tight discipline that has love for the SUGMAD at its heart. This love assures that the spiritual missions of these ECK Masters are carried out in a direct and harmonious manner. If the ECK Adepts can do this, might not also we?

* * *

By the end of March 1981 I had taken the first steps to stop a further slide in my health. Players from the ECK Office had joined an industrial softball league, but after a few practice workouts, several of the original players failed to show up for practice. The team was in need of more players or would be forced to drop out of the league. A player asked if I would like to join the team.

His offer came at just the right time. My rehabilitation called for more strenuous exercise than the brisk walks to work. Maybe softball was the answer.

Two years earlier I had donated my baseball glove and shoes to Goodwill. The new pair of baseball shoes I had bought at a discount store hurt my feet. But most of the team had also bought their shoes there. Somebody passed along this advice: ''Wear two pairs of socks and your feet won't hurt!'' Simple but good advice, and it worked. I was ready to run!

The first day of practice it was pure joy to be on a ball field again. Up until ten years earlier I had been on a fast-pitch team, earning a .511 batting average. I had added to my batting average each year by making a detailed study of other batters and pitchers.

The ECK team was in a slow-pitch league, generally of a lower level of play than fast-pitch, so I expected an easy time of fitting in with the team and earning a regular slot on the playing field. But this turned out to be far from true.

My body had aged ten years since I last played competitive ball, and as I ran, it was all too obvious that my legs were uncommonly weak. Just last summer I had run in the park with my young daughter and had felt strong. But now, two months after my brother's illness had come to light, my physical condition had gone downhill to the point where I needed twelve hours of sleep at night just to drag through the next day.

164

Something was certainly wrong. The leg muscles were sodden and lacked firmness, while the knee joints hurt and an ache came from deep in my bones.

The muscles in my right arm tore loose the first day of practice. They separated as easily as strands of fresh bread dough and caused me a lot of pain. Practice was on Saturday morning; by Sunday it was nearly impossible to roll out of bed. Two weeks later, the leg muscles gave way entirely in the first game as I tried to outrace a grounder to the shortstop. As I ran, a whole bundle of muscles tore away on the front of both thighs, and also in back. My face was drawn in pain as I stumbled the last few steps to first base, and our coach shouted as I hobbled by, ''You OK?''

Nodding, I limped from the field, puzzled at my body's inability to carry out a simple thing like a run of sixty feet.

By the time this first game took place, my arm had already been a limp rag for two weeks. It was impossible to throw the ball much further than sixty feet. This distressed me greatly: I had in the past enjoyed a strong arm through many seasons of play. My weak arm was an embarrassment, and it left no choice but to try out for second base. That position could get by with probably the weakest arm on the field, except for that of first baseman.

There is no need to go into all the details of the lessons learned on the ball field that year, but a number of games made me wish I had stayed home. When fielding a ground ball, my legs were too sore to allow for bending down, so I missed making a play on about half the hits toward my position at second base. An old rule for fielding grounders is to ''get the glove down'' on the ground, but it was impossible to bend that far.

To make up for my weak arm, I developed a smooth double-play throw from second base to first. The move was liquid; unfortunately, my weak throw cancelled out any advantage gained in the economy of motion, but at least it allowed me to be average. The graceful double-play move gave promise of many double plays, but my weak arm made that wishful thinking.

An occasion of bitter humiliation occurred when one of our players hit the ball to right field, and I ran from second base to third. The groundskeeper had overwatered the playing field before the game, and the result was a mud hole between the bases. With better legs under me, it would have been a snap to advance the base. As it turned out, the mud was just too deep and slippery. By the time I had sloshed my way through it, the fielder's throw to third forced me back to second. There I got mired in the mud again, and the second baseman made an easy tag for an out. The frustration was almost too much to handle.

But the most embarrassing moment on the field happened when my health was at its lowest point. This was before all my efforts at exercise had begun to pay off.

The pitcher gave me an unintentional walk to first, and the next batter's sacrifice hit advanced me to second. The batter after that hit a sharp double to deep center field. Our man on third crossed home plate, while I headed around third to try to score another run. But my legs collapsed halfway between third and home, and I fell to the ground utterly spent. So this is what it is like to be old, I thought.

The play on the runner to second was close and involved a lot of shouting as the umpire tried to enforce his "safe" call upon our opponents. Meanwhile, I began to crawl for home plate with my last ounce of strength. The umpire at second base settled the argument in our favor, and the other team began to throw the ball around the infield, getting ready for our next batter. Nobody paid attention while I continued my patient crawl toward home plate.

As I came within a baby's reach of home, the catcher gave me a curious sidelong glance, trying to establish my intentions. Had I been celebrating in the dugout?

By and by, as I inched closer with fixed determination, he figured it out. "Throw the ball! Throw the ball!" he screamed at the pitcher, who held the ball in wonderment, trying to decide what kind of conference the catcher and I might be holding. By the time the pitcher threw the ball to the catcher, I had inched across home plate to score another run and was on my way to the safety of the sidelines.

The odd thing was that hardly anyone had seen this remarkable crawl toward home; everybody's attention was on second base. Concerned teammates were at once pleased that I had scored, but puzzled at the unorthodox way in which it was done.

But as the season wore on, a silver-haired umpire took pity on me. He saw me struggle to run, throw, and field. It got so that a runner ran to first in my stead when I hit the ball. The umpire tried to discourage me from playing on the team and did it by giving indirect examples from his own life.

"Now take me," he said one night as I waited to step into the batter's box. "I quit playing ball at thirty-eight. My legs wouldn't take the beating anymore. And then there was the family. The kids were at a good age to enjoy them, so why should I go out to the ballpark and break a leg? I was too old to take chances like that. Now I ump and get paid for watching the game. Best seat in the house— Play ball!"

The message was clear: Get out now, in one piece.

But his words had no effect on me, and I kept coming to the games. My battle was not with fading youth, but with death— which no one else knew, of course.

Since the umpire could not discourage me, he began to give me pointers on batting. From my low batting average, he assumed this was my first year in softball, which stung my pride to no end. In my best years as a hitter, I had developed excellent bat control. My expertise was singles hit just over the infield, to the other team's weakest side.

The umpire now had two undertakings: to supervise the game with absolute fairness to both teams (the one he was paid for), and to teach me how to bat again. That this might have been a conflict of interests never seemed to have occurred to him. He was at once the impartial field judge and

Good Samaritan.

So while the other team was throwing the ball to each other, he whispered as I came to bat, "Hit it over second. See the hole?" Between his advice and my careful attention to it, we did all right. My batting average began to move into the low .300s, certainly a respectable average. He strutted like a proud poppa each time I reached base, and congratulated me under his breath when I crossed home plate. He was an unusual man who kept my spirits up during some very dark days.

One more thing bears mention before closing this section on softball. When I was at my weakest level of strength, our team ran headlong into a most awesome opponent: huge players from a drayage company. Their bulging muscles were testimony to the fact that they were employees of a company whose specialty was moving heavy equipment. Our team watched in awe as they took the field for pregame batting practice. These players could run, hit, and throw like nothing we had ever seen before.

The game opened, and we took our positions on the field with serious misgivings. Each batter looked bigger and meaner than the one before him. Each was big enough to loft the ball out of the park and into the trees at will. But they liked to hit the ball at us, on the ground, to watch us dodge and run. I felt like a soldier on a Civil War battlefield whose lieutenant has just issued him a ball glove and an order: "Catch the bouncing cannonballs; they could hurt somebody!"

To my great relief, the first few hits went to our third baseman and shortstop. The rough playing field made it treacherous to be caught in the line of fire; a bad bounce might mean the rest of the season on the bench, or worse, in the bleachers with a cast.

Then came my turn to cower in earnest. Nearly half the players on the drayage team batted left-handed, which meant the hits came to the first baseman and to me, on second. For his part, the first baseman hugged first base, afraid to venture out onto the playing field where he might be hurt. His timidity left me, alone, to field the smashing drives to the right side of the infield.

The bats of the left-handed hitters began to boom like cannons. Cannonballs, made up to look like softballs, tore up the field around me as I crouched in quiet desperation behind my glove, trying to be as small a target as possible. Our team was fortunate to suffer no loss greater than that of the game. The other team won handily, and after the game, we joined in the traditional hand-slapping line of losers who congratulate the winners. The evening had only been a mild sedative for them, but we were exultantly alive—grateful for the gift of life.

The loss of that game marked the lowest point of my health. But finally, all the effort of self-discipline began to pay off. My running began to improve: I no longer fell down between bases and could run three bases without making a spectacle of myself. The umpire and I were batting much better, especially with runners on base. That made us both proud beyond words.

A further improvement was the partial healing of my leg muscles. I could now stoop down without pain and field ground balls: I was a ball player at last.

All during this summer of softball, my training for ECK Mastership had again begun to move forward in high gear. But I kept my inner life a carefully guarded secret, for who would understand? Anyway, it is known among initiates to keep such things absolutely to oneself. A candidate for ECK Mastership may not even tell his mate of being selected for advanced training, unless it is with permission from the Living ECK Master.

Our team made it to the play-offs, which were held right before the 1981 ECK World Wide Seminar which was to be in Anaheim, California. Other teams had players with more experience and ability, but we learned fast. We were truly a team; nobody tried to be a star at the expense of his teammates. This unity of spirit made us a well-oiled unit, and we won the early play-off games with little trouble.

But then trouble did come. It was in the form of our old nemesis, the drayage team. They stood between us and second place. The season was at an end, and the long summer of ball playing had put new strength into my body. What would be the outcome of this game with players from Weight Lifters Anonymous?

All ten of us on the starting team had swallowed hard when the play-off schedule pitted them against us. Our first game with them earlier in the season had left wounds in our confidence. We now slunk onto the playing field as if being forced to advance on enemy entrenchments armed only with squirt guns. But a miracle, which none of us had foreseen, was to take place during this game.

For some reason, we were able to catch the cannonballs that exploded from their bats, and to throw out their base runners. We turned several double plays as if we had been raised on them. And during our turn at bat, we hit well-placed shots to the wide open spaces.

Our win was the upset of the season, but our opponents showed style in the gracious way they congratulated us after the game.

The season ended for me then because the World Wide intervened here. The rest of the team went into the final play-offs after the seminar and lost to the first-place team, but did earn second place. A day of celebration.

By the time the World Wide rolled around near the end of October, the long, hard haul of the softball season had served its purpose: It had restored my health to the point where I could accept the Rod of ECK Power and begin my spiritual mission.

That summer stands in my memory as a time of camaraderie, of friendly fellowship with an outstanding group of ECKists who also liked to play ball. The support of our cheering section—spouses and children, and other ECK friends—carried us through the dark times of the early season. All of us, without a doubt, learned our own lessons from that softball season of 1981.

While my outer life was being rebuilt, inner changes were also taking place. The Inner Master had kept up a regular schedule of appearances during my contemplations. The inner was to balance the outer life, which had been in a bad way.

Also that summer, management at the ECK Office, under the direction of Gross, was conducting one of its many employee purges. The reason given for these firings was "economic cutback." Management would allow the staff's size to balloon to around sixty-five people, then, a month later, came the firings. It was like the autumn harvest after the summer growing season. The axe seemed to fall at random, and the turnover of staff personnel was incredibly high.

The production department, where I worked, accounted for a third of the employees. Our people were lighthearted and made jokes whenever anyone in the department got a call to come to the front office.

"It's been good knowing you," was one joke. "Can I have your cup?"

Watching the attitudes of the fired employees was an education. Those who accepted their discharge as the will of ECK, no matter what their feelings might have been about the ability of top management, usually found good jobs. Dave, who lost his place in the printing department, immediately found a better paying job at a large electronics firm. He was offered the highest salary of his career. Even the starting date of his employment was juggled to give him a few extra weeks of vacation time between jobs.

Others, who had been poking sticks at the ineptness of management before they were fired, often ended up with poor jobs or none at all. The latter did not know the art of spiritual survival and were ready to judge everything from

171

their own narrow viewpoint. So the ECK put them into a confining financial position—to fit their confined state of consciousness. Perfect justice, but it was seldom seen that way.

The number of firings at the ECKANKAR Office were uncommonly high at times. Sometimes the general manager himself seemed unaware of the impact of the decisions he carried out. One day the current general manager walked into the printing area and was surprised to see only a handful of us at work on the equipment.

"Where is everybody?" he demanded of the printing manager.

"What do you mean?" the printer snapped back. "You fired them!"

It was commonly accepted that Gross was responsible for most of the firing; the managers just carried out his wishes. The high turnover created a constant strain on staff morale, because employees were kept guessing as to where next month's rent would come from.

For self-protection, I kept myself in a ready frame of mind. If anyone called me in for firing, I could be gone at a moment's notice. My personal belongings were always at hand in the camera room, stored neatly on a shelf. Maybe this detached attitude saved me during the times that my voice of objection was raised too loudly at some of the zany office procedures. Who knows?

But the turmoil in the office was mere child's play in light of my fight with the angel of death. I made the most diligent effort to remain in the body if the spiritual hierarchy wanted my services as the next Living ECK Master. With that goal as a point of reference, I did not place undue attention upon the erratic behavior of management.

By April 3, 1981, the ECK-Vidya gave indications that Gross was still planning to step aside as the Living ECK Master. The only question was when? On this date I saw him in his office on the Causal Plane, where he was putting his things in order. None of the staff paid the least attention to what he was doing at his desk. I went into the office provided for my use and cleaned the desk drawers, arranging the contents into order.

This inner experience was the ECK-Vidya giving a picture of the future: Gross was clearly ready to vacate his position. He had provided a desk for my use, but it was badly in need of cleaning. This was confirmation that my first project, which was to last the better part of five years, was to revamp the whole outer structure of ECKANKAR.

But all that was to come much later. In the meantime, I had to last through another six months of testing until October 22, 1981. Would that day see the fulfillment of my spiritual dreams, or would it be another day of bitter disappointment, as in 1980?

Only time could tell.

The Living ECK Master had asked that I write my own version of the ECK introductory brochure. "Do it as if you were the Living ECK Master," he said. "I'm serious."

9

From the Master's Chair

A hurdle we face on the journey to God is whether a Master is a help or hindrance to our spiritual unfoldment.

By the time an individual comes to ECK, he has seen it all. Religious leaders at all levels have tried to convince him that they alone can help him in his progress toward truth. But events usually prove them wrong. They have no more spiritual power than the seeker himself. He finds out the hard way the meaning of "the blind leading the blind." Why should the Living ECK Master be any different from them?

However, by now I was past that stage of doubting. There are masters, and there are *Masters*. Even the power of Jesus turned out to be nothing more than an emotional force. After he left this earthly theater, the Light and Sound of God was no longer a vital force in the Christian church. Light and Sound were replaced by faith, belief, and feeling. These qualities, while good starting points on the road to God, will never lead to God.

Is the Mahanta, the Inner Master, just another mediator between God and man? Is the Mahanta a latent state of consciousness inside a person that can be tapped at will?

175

Even by one still under the control of the five passions of the mind?

It is not. A paradox is that those people who are least ready for the high consciousness of God are certain they are the most ready to receive it. But they are like monkeys who pat their own heads as a substitute for love from another.

The Shariyat-Ki-Sugmad, Book Two, makes it very clear what the role of the Mahanta is in the seeker's life. It says: "If there were power alone in the name of the SUGMAD, or in his secret name, surely those who know would have great influence. But this proves that power alone does not lie in the Word; it is in the Mahanta, the Living ECK Master."

Since youth my spiritual training had been directed toward accepting the Rod of ECK Power. But the road was a long, uncertain one. The challenge is first to reach the heights of God, but thereafter, one's disciplines play an ever greater role in his life. The reason for this is that the Kingdom of Heaven must be rewon every day.

All these considerations were always at the edge of my consciousness. An individual's love for God must be all-consuming. Life then leaves him no choice but to put aside all interests of self-gain for the pursuit of God Awareness.

How much do I want God? This is the question each person in ECK must often ask himself.

A personal example from 1974 is my interview with the general manager of the ECKANKAR Office. When he asked me to work in the camera department, my only objective was to serve the ECK. What were my salary requirements? I told him my current salary and also that my first wife was still recovering from a stay in the intensive care ward during the premature birth of our daughter. Both my wife and daughter were still on special medication.

The manager offered me less than my present salary. But I knew that the ECK would provide whatever was needed for our survival. (There were, however, times of doubt.)

So I accepted his offer and drove to the ECK Office in Las Vegas with only the will to serve ECK. The Office had not yet moved to California.

Not everyone feels this strongly about service to God. A recent applicant for a position at the ECK Office gave two reasons for the job. First, it would be an opportunity to expand his business knowledge. Second, the job was a good way to serve ECK. The reasons are out of order: material interest is first; service to ECK, second. How long will it take one to reach the heights of God by walking backward?

A seemingly minor point on a résumé, but a telling one.

The softball team in 1981 was afterwork leisure, but most of my time and attention was usually on other things.

The Inner Master kept up his regular visits at night to shape me to have the right feelings and attitudes to be an ECK Master. On May 25, 1981, he called together a group of Higher Initiates on the inner planes. This occasion was to teach me more about letting others help in the work of ECK, but also, to cut down on pontification.

The spiritual message is the spiritual message. It may seem to outsiders that the Living ECK Master presents the message in a pompous or dogmatic way, but he must still give out the teachings to people as the ECK directs him. That is the meaning of the term "clear channel." There are limits to how the message is given, and I had to learn them.

Presently the initiates settled into the comfortable sofas in the meeting room, which looked like a living room. The Inner Master took the floor. First, he introduced me to the others in a quiet, conversational voice. "Here's Sri Harold Klemp," he said. I made a mental note to see if he would later introduce anyone else with that title of spiritual respect. In ECK, it is reserved for the ECK Masters.

His introduction was my cue to address the group. I

started to speak, weakly at first, but then turned up the volume so that my voice would carry above the murmur of conversations adrift in the room. Just as my oration was building up steam, the Master broke in on it.

"Oh, here are a couple of other folks!" he said, and several tardy people shuffled in.

The interruption scattered my thoughts. When the last person had settled into a chair, I again launched into the welcoming address. The idea was to quickly steer the talk to the topic of ECK seminars, the purpose for this meeting. But the Inner Master again interrupted my sermon.

"Let's hear from John for his impressions about seminars," he said.

Picking up on his lead, I chimed in, "Yes, let's do that!"

What was the lesson of this experience? Include others who want to help in the work of ECK, and *do not pontificate!* The experience was humbling.

Experiences like the one above take place in heaven, but it is not the antiquated heaven of Christianity. People in heaven also live, move, and have their being—in modern suits and dresses.

In general, the major religions locate their heavens on the Mental Plane, the fourth heaven. These religions include Christianity, the Jewish religion, Islam, Buddhism, and Hinduism. Of course, the divergence of consciousness in any major religion is so wide that minor offshoots establish their resting place on the Astral Plane, where they feel more at home.

Any group that harks back to animism gravitates to the Astral Plane, the second heaven. This is the lowest of the heavens, nearest to the Physical Plane. Animism is the doctrine that attributes conscious life, by way of spirits, to natural objects of nature.

Others who make their homes on the Astral Plane at death are people who break away from mainline Christianity. Such factions include the Holiness Movement that rocked the Methodist church between 1880 and 1900. This movement, a reaction to the growing formalism of the mother church, offered a return to "heart religion." Although it set its sights on the Astral Plane, instead of the Mental, it was an emotional tide that met the needs of many people.

The Pentecostal movement, a contemporary offshoot, is also highly emotional in nature. Its followers usually find homes on the Astral Plane at death.

This simply points to the many levels of heaven that exist because of differences in spiritual unfoldment. All heavens are right for the people who go there, or they would not be there. It is like the inscription on a coffee mug that says: "No matter where you go, there you are." The spiritual law is simple and forthright about such things as the destinations of people at death of the body.

It makes one wonder why religions engage in declared and undeclared wars on each other. The excuse is saving Souls. But saving them from what?

The Living ECK Master breezed in and out of the ECK Office all that summer of 1981. On occasion he would stop to ask how the work flow was going in the printing department.

It was Friday, July 3, the day before the big Independence Day weekend. A new press was in-house, and it required extra time to make test plates for the pressman in charge of it. That morning I was called away from my camera duties for a brief meeting of the ECK Literary Panel, for which I was the office correspondent to the field. The panel was to review manuscripts for publication by IWP Publishing.

Right before lunch I took a break from printing to catch up on letters to authors. The ECK Literary Panel meeting that morning had eaten up valuable time, and my plans were to work through lunch. Just then a manager ran into the room. In his hand was the rough copy for a new ECK introductory brochure. Would I review it and write up an evaluation in an hour?

"No hurry," he said, "but I'm leaving for the airport right after lunch."

So I put the letters to the side, checked my watch, and got to work on the brochure. Just as I got absorbed in the brochure, the Living ECK Master walked in and sat at the light table. He was in high spirits.

"Are you planning a big weekend for the Fourth (of July)?" he asked. He paused a moment, then said with a laugh, "Or a little one?" But I had been too busy during the week to give the weekend any thought yet.

Then he asked, "How's the work load in printing?"

It had been a very heavy schedule all summer, but I did not mention that. Printing took up only a fraction of my time, since many side projects had been put into my lap, too. One of these assignments was to review initiate reports, which took more than two hours a day. That was to be done at home on my own time. But whenever possible, I took advantage of momentary quiet spells in the printing department and read them in the privacy of the darkroom.

No one else was to be told of this letter-reading task, which was a part of my service to ECK. More specifically, it was training for ECK Mastership. It was imperative that I become versed in the spiritual problems of ECK initiates. Soon their inner lives would be my responsibility.

I was struck by the sincerity of the letter writers. Most spoke from the beautiful and sacred place in their hearts. Running through these letters was a stream of testimony to personal experiences in the Sound and Light of God. Many accounts were of meetings with the elusive ECK Masters, either in the physical world or in the spiritual realms.

There were also testimonies of spiritual healings. The number of people around the globe with similar ECK experiences was an eye-opening revelation.

As I read more of these private letters over the passing weeks, I developed the ability to tell what was in a letter by merely touching the envelope. A letter with good news, or no problems, carries a much different rate of vibration from one with disappointment or sorrow. When the pressure of time required a faster reading speed, I employed this touch method.

Letters from people whose lives were in balance I put aside in order that requests for spiritual aid might have top priority.

Reading such letters of karma meant using absolute detachment. I jotted a brief note to the Living ECK Master about the contents of a letter, then wiped everything from my consciousness. That is what it means to be a clear channel for ECK. It was necessary to step out of the way so that no obstruction could bar a spiritual healing.

So all this was in my mind when the Living ECK Master asked me about the work load in printing. I said the ECK was helping me through it.

He got up from his stool and stopped by the door. "We'll have to sit down and talk sometime after I come back from the European Seminar," he said. "I don't want to keep you from work." Then he left.

By the time I finished my review of the new ECK brochure, the lunch hour was over. The printers were drifting back to work, and they wanted more test plates for the new press. So I put the ECK Literary Panel correspondence away, hoping for a chance to get the mail current before the weekend.

That summer of 1981 saw such a heavy flow of work that I hardly ever took off for lunch anymore. This did nothing for my weak health. Later that afternoon I caught up with the mail for the ECK Literary Panel. It meant mailing back rejected manuscripts to authors. Others got better news:

their manuscript had gone to a higher review. After the mail was done and the pressmen satisfied, I finished the month-end Literary Panel report to management.

Rest would be first on the list for this Fourth of July weekend.

The camera work, the initiate reports, the Literary Panel, the reviews of brochures and projects, and the other duties, all required a high degree of time management. Just when it seemed that one more job would do me in, here came the job.

The scheduler came with a special request. In two weeks he was going on vacation. He and the printing manager had taken a vote on who would fill his shoes during his absence—me. He was in charge of routing printing jobs through the office: a full-time job all by itself. Another load to handle. But the ECK must have something in it for me to learn. What could I do but say yes?

The new ECK brochure had a hard time getting off the ground. In mid-July the general manager asked me into his office to give him my ideas on it. The Living ECK Master came into the room and made the suggestion that I write my own version of the brochure.

"Do it as if you were the Living ECK Master," he said. "I'm serious."

An hour later he made a point of it again when I bumped into him by accident at the mailboxes. I had left the meeting with the general manager and gone back to my camera duties. It was necessary to deliver a memo to someone's mailbox near the reception area. Gross and his wife were just leaving the building.

In a firm voice, he said, "I meant it before. Write as if you are sitting in my chair. I want to see the brochure personally; it's not for anyone else."

As he hurried toward the exit, I passed a few words with

the receptionist, standing by in case Gross needed anything else. As he reached the door, he shouted, "Harold?" I was out of sight behind a partition. I looked around the corner, and he added, "What would you write for the uninitiated? What can ECK do for them?"

Then he left.

I spent all weekend putting down ideas that came through from the ECK. It required an entirely new viewpoint to look at the spiritual needs of people from the Master's chair. Getting ideas was only a third of the project: They needed sorting and then had to be written into copy.

But when it rains, it pours. That weekend was the one my in-laws picked for a visit. My wife's parents came Friday, right after work. Only after they had returned to their motel late at night did I get a chance to gather material for the brochure. The morning came quickly, and I had had only a few hours of sleep. Saturday afternoon came another surprise. Now my wife's sister and her two daughters dropped by. They stayed the remainder of the day but left that night.

I have noticed this trend many times since then. When the ECK is flowing strongly through Its channel, people are drawn to the individual. It is an unconscious attraction, but they are there to drink of the ECK. But they would also be the first to discount the idea, especially if they are of a spiritual background other than ECK. An ECK channel learns that this is part of the selfless service he can offer to the SUGMAD—his time.

All the relatives left Saturday night. I worked all day Sunday, until two a.m. on Monday morning. At 5:30 a.m. I got up to catch the bus for work. Little sleep.

That was how most of the summer went. The ECK pulled and stretched me until it seemed impossible to call up any more energy for another project. All the while I was sick, trying to find a way to recover my health.

This is what makes it so laughable to get a letter from a "minimaster". He is a person who thinks he is the next

Living ECK Master. If there were one measure for an individual in training for the ECK Mastership, it would be this: never to speak of his spiritual preparation to anyone. Especially never in writing. That sums up the law of silence. None of these minimasters has gone through the hardships of testing required of a candidate for the Vairagi Order's top echelons. If he had, he would not act this way. He is only a vain fellow who wants a following. Whatever qualities, disciplines, or training it takes to become the spiritual leader of ECKANKAR are quite beyond his understanding.

The project of writing the ECK brochure from the Master's viewpoint was a whole new concept to me. It was a real effort to learn the skill of seeing life from the spiritual heights.

Soul Travelers to the Far Country are taught in a manner such as I was. A problem of the day serves as instructional fodder at night, for learning in the dream state or by Soul Travel.

On July 19, 1981, I went out of the body during contemplation. I was a truck driver moving his rig through the streets of a metropolis. This took place on the Astral Plane, but I left the Astral body and rose into the Causal consciousness. In the Soul body, I had left the driver's body behind in the truck, under remote control, and rose to the height of a skyscraper for an overview of the city. It was hard to steer the truck from up there.

The feeling was like being perched on the tip of the Washington Monument. But I was unafraid, despite the great height, because as Soul I was an indestructible unit of awareness. I parked the truck by remote control then came back down into my body to walk the grounds of the city's Temple of Golden Wisdom.

This inner experience was a demonstration of what it

takes to be the Living ECK Master, who regularly goes out of the body, into a higher state of consciousness, to get an overview of a problem brought to him. The trick is to do that and stay awake. It is cumbersome to have to enter a trance and lose control of the body each time the Master partakes of the Mahanta Consciousness.

The difference between one Living ECK Master and another is the way in which he relates with the supreme consciousness of the Mahanta. The spiritual leader of ECK may be either a Mahanta or a Living ECK Master. If he is the Mahanta, it means the ECK passes through him constantly at the highest level. One who is the Living ECK Master operates within the Mahanta Consciousness. The difference is first in the severity of the training. The Mahanta, the Living ECK Master (the full title) has undergone a life of hardship and upheaval since his tutoring under the ECK Masters began as a child.

There are no words adequate to describe the tests, undertakings, and sufferings he must endure to prepare him for the greatness to come. This preparation occurs on both the inner and outer planes.

The second distinction to make between a Mahanta and a Living ECK Master who operates within the Mahanta Consciousness is one of power. The full power of the ECK is at the disposal of the Mahanta at all times. The Living ECK Master may call upon the power when needed. Each of these ECK Masters is at a level far superior to that of a priest, rabbi, or pastor. No comparison is possible between the ECK Masters and teachers of other orders.

Nor can an ECK initiate correctly determine the stature of the spiritual leader of ECK, because the Mahanta state of being is completely outside his league to judge. It would be like asking a child whether George Washington or Abraham Lincoln was the greatest president of the United States. The child might make a guess, but does not have the knowledge or experience to do more than hazard an opinion. His guess would have little foundation.

185

Yet initiates make judgments all the time about one Master over another. But what is their yardstick to make such a judgment?

After parking the truck by remote control, I started across a lawn and headed toward the building complex that comprised this Temple of Golden Wisdom. It was a branch of the main temple at Askleposis. An arsonist was setting fire to kindling against the side of a building. Several of us pedestrians took up the chase that led through several classrooms and captured him. The others took him into custody.

The meaning of this segment of the inner experience was given through the ECK-Vidya, the science of prophecy. The arsonist represented the shortsighted higher initiates who had left ECK in 1980. This experience gave the perspective that their attempt to set ECKANKAR aflame had failed, a finding supported by history.

The ECK-Vidya shows those things that are of concern to us. Too often, however, the initiate has no interest in developing this skill, which is perfectly all right. But neither should he complain that life gives no warnings of situations that will harm him. The ECK always gives a warning through the ECK-Vidya of those things that concern our spiritual unfoldment. Always.

As I walked the halls of the temple, a chela came up to ask a question. He had been having a most difficult time carrying out a certain spiritual technique given in a textbook. Out of frustration he had invented another one, which worked well for him. Was he doing the right thing?

"By all means," I assured him, "do whatever works for you." He wanted an outer confirmation of the direction given to him by the Inner Master. Now he was happy in the knowledge that his invention was a safe spiritual move.

The Ninth Initiation came on July 22, 1981. Initiations

in ECK beyond the Eighth are given only on the inner planes. Very few initiates ever go further into the God Worlds than the Eighth Plane. It is a difficult road to follow.

The Inner Master studied me for a while. "This initiation's going to be a handful for you." He kept on talking in a light vein, but his words made me tremble: "Yes, this one's a real handful!" Then the ECK Current rushed into me.

"Ah, yes, I see what you mean," I said, giving the Master a knowing look.

The initiation had begun, even though the Master kept chatting outwardly. I trembled again, thinking of the future. It was little comfort to know that all of the ECK Masters had also once faced this "Terror of God." Many had advanced far beyond this level of Mastership. That thought gave me the courage to explore more fully the Agam Lok, for I was now a Maulani, a dweller of that plane. The first time I had come here was as a visitor during my experience of 1970.

The spiritual planes, or heavens, are unlike the layers of rock in geology. These worlds are in a creation of no time and no space. Therefore, they are states of being that melt into each other, leaving no hard lines, such as boundary lines, to show where one world begins or another ends. And the clearest Light of God shines in them. The heavens of the lower worlds are dark places if a comparison were possible.

Two days after the Ninth Initiation, the Inner Master brought me all kinds of material on the administration of ECKANKAR. I was to digest it. There was so much of it that I felt like an ant before a towering mountain. I gave it my best effort to wade through it, to rearrange procedures for getting the administrative details in order.

This load of training was the last straw. I looked at the Master and asked wearily, "Is it necessary?"

"Yes, it must be done."

Then he patted my shoulder for reassurance and added, "You're doing just fine." That was a comfort to hear, because my outer life was racing along at triple speed, too.

I am used to hard work; my parents raised me to it. The work in the ECK Office was not the manual labor of the farm, but it required mental alertness and never-ending hustle. It took another week to write the copy for the new introductory brochure. A great number of manuscripts came through the ECK Literary Panel for review, and these reviews were expected to be done at home on our own time.

In addition, I was an Arahata at the ECK Center in Mountain View, California; this time for a new *Letters to a Chela* class. Then there was softball twice a week—both a workout and a game—to restore my body from the health crisis of the first quarter of the year. Besides this, I was engaged in confidential projects for the Living ECK Master. In printing, I often worked on through the morning and afternoon breaks—and lunch—just to keep the presses on schedule under impossible deadlines.

On the home front, our family life was practically nil. There was precious little time for my wife and daughter. This was the schedule: home on the train by 6:30 p.m., two to three hours of office work, dinner, bed, and up at 5:30 to catch the bus. The schedules for travel made it more convenient to ride the bus in the morning and take the train at night.

But my wife had her own busy schedule. She was taking night classes at a community college, was a volunteer for a local political candidate, had a home business selling household products, and worked with a temporary agency in the daytime. Despite our heavy schedules, one of us was always at home with our daughter after school. It took extraordinary planning.

* * *

My ideas about Soul Travel and its purpose when I first got into ECKANKAR in 1967 had now moved into a broader understanding of what Soul Travel really was. My whole purpose then was to get out of the body, to flee the restrictions of military service, to go to the other side of the fence where the grass was greener: home. In other words, Soul Travel represented the Great Escape. I did not want to face up to my responsibilities; it was that simple. Soul Travel—if it worked, and I was not sure at that time that it would—might provide an acceptable means to escape the life I had made for myself by enlisting in the Air Force. The distasteful alternative was compulsory induction into the Army, a foregone conclusion because of the Vietnam War.

Soul Travel was an acceptable way to go AWOL in spirit and avoid the bitter penalties that come with real physical desertion.

How did my understanding of Soul Travel expand as I developed in spiritual maturity? For one thing, I saw that travel into the inner worlds was not to be for self-gratification. It was to be in service of God. This gave meaning to my inner life, without which I would have spent my whole life in giving chase to empty dreams.

Saints who went into seclusion in order to receive the Light of God, but did not return the love in deeds of charity, were not saints in the true sense. A papal decree can give someone the name of saint, but by their deeds shall they be known. God did not intend for the illuminated individual to hide away from truth seekers and refuse to pass along the methods of spiritual liberation. Especially as there are always some with the inner preparation to receive the methods.

Such acts of selfishness reveal a spiritual adolescence. This adolescence is the very condition that God once sent

189

us, as Souls, into the lower worlds to overcome.

What did my inner travels show in the days before I received the Rod of ECK Power? The Inner Master had me acting out the role of leader to ECKists who often made improbable plans to present ECK to people.

For example, during a Soul Travel experience in early August, initiates had set up booths for the sale of food and crafts. They were raising funds for the ECK Center. The Master said to me, "Why don't you step in here and help out?" That meant, do something! But what? I sat back and watched, but no customers came to the ECKists' booths.

I called an impromptu meeting of the initiates. "Why is no one coming to your stands?"

No sooner had I asked the question than people came in such droves that there was no time for the meeting. When this wave of people had left, I called another meeting in the slack time. Again, flocks of customers descended upon the booths as before.

What was the lesson in this Soul Travel experience? It was the phenomenon that marketing people have observed for years, but not understood. Sincere planning for growth is itself a stimulus for growth, even before the plan can be put into action. Invisible causes (forces) are set into motion, and the public responds to them in advance of the outer sales effort. This is a demonstration in the business world of the spiritual dynamic: As above, so below.

Whatever can be conceived of as thought on the Mental Plane can manifest on the Physical Plane, although often in a different form than expected.

This highlights the need for making plans when giving service to ECK. If a plan fails to bring the desired results, the ECK leader calls a meeting of the initiates who have a proven record of accomplishment in their own lives. The plans of this group are more likely to work than those

which are generated merely by feelings (the Astral factor).
For instance, "I let the ECK flow in the introductory talk
and you could just *feel* the ECK."

The feeling power has its place, because it gives life to
plans. But action based solely on feelings and not planning
is usually short-lived and thus ineffective.

That is the way my Soul Travel expectations had
changed from the time I came into ECK, until this moment—the eleventh hour of full Mastership in the Vairagi
Order.

By the time the middle of August had rolled around, I
was weary in body and spirit. The ECK Masters accepted
me as an equal. Travel with them was like a refreshing
breath of spring air.

The ECK Masters usually go about their own missions,
hardly ever coming into contact with each other unless it is
for special occasions. They know their assignments, which
are coordinated through the office of the current Living
ECK Master. There is little reason for them to be in contact with each other. They are God-Realized individuals.
Their attention is on the SUGMAD, and this has them in
agreement with each other. It is an automatic part of high
consciousness.

They have mastered the problems of the little self, the
ego. There is no need to desire positions of power or to be
in control. They know what service is theirs to give, and
give it they do, agreeably and quietly.

A small band of ECK Masters met on the inner planes on
August 19 to discuss plans for the passing of the Rod of
ECK Power at the World Wide Seminar in Anaheim, California. The date this was to occur was October 22, the
traditional date in the Vairagi Order for this most sacred of
rituals.

The ECK Masters in attendance on the nineteenth were

Rebazar Tarzs (in a maroon robe), Fubbi Quantz (in a white one), and Dap Ren (in blue shirt and slacks). When the meeting came to a close, Dap Ren turned to me and said, "Come with me on a long journey to the Himalayas."

Rebazar pointed at the distant peaks and shrugged. "He's already been to the Katsupari Monastery and Agam Des. Why not something new?"

The ECK-Vidya was giving insight into my spiritual mission. Dap Ren's invitation was to go to old places, places well familiar in our travels. Rebazar was saying that the missions of Peddar Zaskq and Dap Ren had explored these areas. I was to bring the high ECK teachings down into the everyday lives of people. So our journey was to the lowlands by the seashore.

The lowlands had a greater population because life was easier than in the forbidding mountains. Only a few hardy travelers had the stamina necessary for survival in the wilds. This was therefore the ECK-Vidya restating a part of my mission to come.

What were my expectations in the closing days of my anonymity? One day, printer; next day, spiritual leader of the most vital path to God known. After plans fell apart the previous year for my acceptance of the ECK Mastership, I kept myself tempered with a respectful, wait-and-see attitude.

It was now the beginning of September 1981. Summer was over, Labor Day weekend was a few days hence. Schools were about to open for the fall semester.

On the inner planes, I was surrounded by snakes in my workplace—snakes of every color, size, and description. I pushed and pulled people out of harm's way. No snakebite ever found me.

What did this inner experience mean? The ECK gave

warning in this of treachery at the ECK Office. It meant to keep away from personalities and stick to the business in the camera area. It was not a time to be a victim of spiteful jealousies.

But things were going strange in other places, too. A shocking event happened two days after the dream. Two respected Higher Initiates from nearby Redwood City, California, were shot in their apartment. The couple were planning for a quiet evening at home when two men knocked on the door. The woman had words with them, became angry, and ordered them away.

In response, they returned through an unlocked sliding glass door, yelled for the couple to get on the floor, then killed the man and wounded the woman. The next day two men were placed under arrest for the crime.

But the ECKist community was in shock. Why had not the Master given them protection? Even a warning? Where was the special power of direction in ECKANKAR?

They did not understand the effects of the woman's anger, which blocked her inner hearing and set up a chain reaction of events that need not have taken place. The whole incident was a direct result of her flash of anger.

The concerns of the ECKists were not unlike those of people who had seen Jesus heal the sick. But the passage of time saw the healed succumb to the Angel of Death by some other means. The early followers of Jesus were also torn by the paradox of a divine power that failed to treat all people, across the board, but only selected ones. And of those healed, some died a few years later. What was special about the healings of Jesus if they were not permanent?

Similar questions about the verity of the ECK teachings were thus raised by the apparently senseless attack on these two ECKists.

It was a disquieting period in the month and a half before I was to receive the Rod of ECK Power.

Would that day ever come?

Many did not know it, but public handshaking, as the means of giving the Darshan, would soon be a thing of the past.

10

A Blank Page in History

With all the running around at work, teaching Satsang classes, time for my family, and the physical therapy of softball, where was there room for spirituality? ECK is probably the most active path to God that one can imagine. That is true only for the real devotees of the Holy Spirit, however. Any path is what the individual makes of it.

Did my hectic schedule leave time for the Spiritual Exercises of ECK? Always. But I had to fit them in. Before I married and had a family, it was easy to spend most of the night in contemplation. I would lie down in bed, tuck myself in well for comfort, then shut my eyes and chant my secret word or HU. Every time there was an experience with the Sound or Light of ECK, I switched on a bedside lamp and wrote down in my dream journal whatever had happened.

A fact of good dream or Soul Travel recall is the importance of writing down the experience as soon as it happens. That takes discipline.

The body can be persuaded to move into the disciplined response of opening its eyes, groping for the light switch and pen, and recording the spiritual occasion. But it does take strong willpower to start doing this. Nevertheless, the rewards are worth the trouble. Often, when I read a journal entry the following morning, it was amazing to see what details I had captured in the night. If I tried to wait for morning to record an experience, my mind by then was usually as blank as a whitewashed wall.

When I was single, the only thing that really prevented me from writing an entry in my journal was self-discipline: Would I get up and do it?

Marriage changed a lot of things. Now there were new things to consider. Who can rest when the light switch is constantly being flipped on during the wee hours to write notes in a journal? That is one way to ruin a relationship. It can also be a problem if one of the couple insists on sitting cross-legged on the bed for half an hour before bedtime, lost in the rapture of contemplation. So I found that marriage required some basic changes in how to do the spiritual exercises.

For one thing, it meant using more ingenuity. During contemplation I used to put a pillow over my head to block out noise. But that sort of behavior ruffles a marriage. As a consequence it was necessary to divide my attention equally between spiritual and family needs by staying half awake until my wife fell asleep. *Then* came the exercises.

Sometimes ingenuity called for changing the spiritual exercises to another time. For instance, when a trying day at work compelled me to realign myself with the ECK, I asked my family for privacy and retired into the bedroom for contemplation. One can keep up his spiritual exercises if he really has a mind to do it.

In spite of the frenzied calendar of daily life, I was actually living a spiritual life. There was no time to sit under a pipal tree like Buddha to await illumination. Nor was there the leisure of Krishnamurti, who got the Astral consciousness while under the pepper tree. I would gladly have settled for an hour under any old tree. But that was not to be.

* * *

What is the saving grace of Soul? The ability to keep Its attention directly upon the SUGMAD no matter what. October 22, 1980, had dealt me a staggering blow. Paul Twitchell's prophecy of 1970 saw me as the leader of ECK, but so far that prediction was a big zero. Was I a minimaster, one of the deluded ones who imagines, without cause, that he is to be the next Living ECK Master?

Whenever that thought tried for a foothold in my mind, I immediately switched my attention right to the SUGMAD again. Weren't there enough things trying to ensure my defeat? Why feed such an attitude, even for a moment? Had all my dreams for ECK Mastership been a grand delusion?

Strike that from the record!

OK, then, where is some proof of this supposed Mastership? Has anybody asked you lately to be the Living ECK Master? No? See what I mean?

But, said my mind, the inner experiences had shown me in the Master's role for a number of years already. Remember those dreams?

Hogwash! replied common sense. Inner experiences without the outer validation make you just another minimaster. Proof! Where's the proof! You will need a stronger argument than inner revelation alone to gain the Mastership. Why not forget all this nonsense about God Consciousness?

Then came proof. On September 16, 1981, the opportunity came once again to serve the SUGMAD and present the ECK message as ITS chief agent. By now I was soft clay in the hands of Spirit. My own will had been dashed about so much that nothing mattered anymore. Let Thy will be done, O Lord! The only purpose left in life was service to God, in whatever way I could find.

I was now pursuing my spiritual goal with all my heart and being. My desire had changed from *getting* God Consciousness to *giving* my life in service to God. That was the turning point.

September 16 had started out like any other day in the camera department. No better or worse than hundreds of other such days. It was 4:30 p.m., a half hour before quitting time. The negatives for a book in production lay before me on the light table, a layout sheet beside them. Planning, and lost in thought, I was nudged into awareness by a soft voice. The Living ECK Master had entered the room and found a stool before I was aware of his presence.

"How would you like a new job?" he asked.

"Sure," I said, without hesitation. Whenever the ECK speaks of a duty through Its channel, the Living ECK Master, the best thing is to agree to the assignment, no matter how unworthy one may feel. There will be plenty of time later to worry about how to do it. "Sure!" was hardly the most memorable acceptance speech in the history of ECKANKAR, but it did the job. Upon reflection, I added, "If you see that it is best."

The Living ECK Master sat huddled on the stool, his brows knit in thought. "We really shouldn't talk about it here." He shot a glance at the open door, where anyone might have walked in at any moment.

"We could go into the darkroom," I suggested.

He hesitated, then said, "All right."

Quickly we walked into the most secure of the darkrooms, shut the door, and turned on the light. This darkroom was the perfect place for a private meeting: It was soundproof. The walls of the room were a flat off-white to cut down stray reflections of light for camera work. The double bank of fluorescent lights on the ceiling turned the room into a brilliant white.

He asked whether I would be willing to accept the position of the Living ECK Master. "But before you decide," he said, "talk it over with your wife. You have a lovely family, and I don't want to break it up." This sounded like an exact replay of our conversation in 1980.

Many things were said that won't be mentioned here.

The meeting took from 4:30 p.m. until shortly after five. This is one of those blank pages in history that has no words sufficient to fill it. But he wanted me to have his private phone number, and we walked up to his office. Several staff members, ready to go home, were still in the corridors as we passed.

The Living ECK Master's wife was in his office when we arrived. She told him the phone number, and he jotted it down on a piece of paper, with his initials.

"Just call anytime something comes up," he said.

I took the slip of paper and stumbled back to the camera room for my jacket. There was still time to catch the next bus for home at Marsh Manor, a small shopping mall several blocks away.

He had given his permission to discuss this with my wife, since it concerned her future. When I came home, she was ready to shop for groceries across the street.

"The offer from last year still stands," I said, telling her of the conversation with the Living ECK Master. "I'm still under consideration, but he wants your feelings, too." After some discussion about the privilege and blessing of serving the SUGMAD in this capacity, she agreed to the conditions. She knew that our family life would never be the same: It would prove to be more challenging in ways impossible to describe.

After dinner I called Gross to tell him of my decision and my wife's agreement with it. It seemed a long walk to the phone, longer than in 1980, when I had made a similar call to him. That had been a dry run. Would this be one too? The phone was really only two steps from my chair at the kitchen table, but the distance seemed to span eternity. I thought long and hard as my fingers dialed his number. This simple act of placing a phone call would throw my life into the greatest turmoil.

When he answered, I said, "My wife says it's OK. She made up her own mind." Earlier, in the darkroom, he had offered to meet us at a restaurant for dinner. Now I said that we would be glad to accept the invitation. Whenever it works out, he said. Probably over the weekend or next week. He would let us know.

September 16 had thus been a momentous day, nearly an exact duplicate of a similar one in 1980. This time, could there be a better ending?

Two nights later I was in Los Altos, California, at an Evening with ECK. Gross had called my wife in the meantime to ask what kind of food we liked.

"Harold's system is sensitive," she said.

"Aren't ours all? How about *Mama's* in Stanford Mall?" he asked, naming a fashionable restaurant. The time was set for 7:30 p.m. on Saturday night. "Come casual," he said before hanging up.

Saturday, September 19—the spiritual current of ECK was flowing through me in powerful waves. But where was there time to recline under a pipal or pepper tree in anticipation of receiving the glory of God? Instead, I had an 8 a.m. appointment at a K-Mart store in San Jose that was running a special sale on tires. The front ones on our car were worn out. Today could not be given over to the solitude of meditation, but much of it was to be spent on the freeway and in a service station. The whole thing struck me as ironic and humorous. What might Buddha or Krishnamurti think of spirituality like this?

With new front tires on the car, I took a drive to Stanford Shopping Mall to find the location of *Mama's* restaurant. It was an elegant place with crystalline windows. I noted the best roads to it, then drove home. The rest of the day was spent in doing laundry, writing, and pacing the floor.

Evening finally came. A friend was gracious enough to babysit our daughter while we were at dinner. My wife and I drove to *Mama's* early. A clock in the tower near the front of the restaurant said 7:05, but our reservations weren't until 7:30 p.m. To pass time, we strolled around the shops in the mall. Fifteen minutes later my wife spotted the Living ECK Master and his wife, Sirpa, coming from the parking lot across the street. He wore a long-sleeved blue dress shirt open at the collar, a beige sport jacket over it. His wife, a native of Norway, was equally well-dressed.

Once inside the restaurant he checked with the waiter, who said a table would be ready in a few minutes. In the meantime, Gross suggested freshly squeezed orange juice. After the waiter showed us to our table, I ordered halibut. This was a once-in-a-lifetime meal, but I had no appetite for it.

During the meal, the Living ECK Master outlined the freedoms and responsibilities of the spiritual leader of ECKANKAR. In passing, he said that the testing for ECK Mastership this time had begun with sixty or seventy candidates. But one by one they had stepped aside for one reason or another.

A consideration was how I would work into my new role. My travel schedule might include the major seminars, he said. In November, Don Ginn and Helen Baird were to go to New Zealand, Australia, and Singapore to conduct a Higher Initiates' training. Would I like to join them? He said my wife and daughter were welcome to go along. However, when November came they stayed home: Both were in school. Three weeks on the road would have thrown them hopelessly behind in their studies.

Writing was another topic of discussion. Much new ECK material could be put into writing, if I planned to put my efforts there. Again, the choice was mine.

The freedom and responsibilities he outlined were awesome in scope. Yet I wore the prospect of service with much more ease than last year, when this subject of Mastership had come up initially.

In addition, he asked for permission to read, at the coming seminar, my letter about the initiation on the Altar of Light. This was an experience from the spring of 1978. In it, Fubbi Quantz accompanied me to the SUGMAD. A critic of the account later said it sounded like so many

201

other stories about people with this kind of experience. Of course, he never had any experience himself with the Sound or Light, so he reduced it to the lowest common denominator: his own want of knowledge.

Anyone who has ever had the experience of God knows the futility of trying to describe the indescribable in words. The state of God Consciousness is simply what it is.

One who has this gift of the SUGMAD accepts it with loving gratitude. Can any human critic invalidate the All-ness of God? The vanity of the human race never stops to blush. But the dust of mortal man adds to the fields of earth, while the SUGMAD remains forever—the final testimony of truth.

The Initiation of the Altar of Light was quite different from my experience in the spring of 1970. The latter was my first real taste of the awful majesty of God, and the problem then was the heavy karma still on my books. The vast disparity between the pure Sound Current and the impurities around me in the Soul body caused a terrible reaction. That story will be told elsewhere.

Back at the restaurant table the Living ECK Master had given my wife the Seventh Initiation. After that, the conversation returned to the Passing of the Rod of ECK Power. In essence, the Living ECK Master was going to pass the Rod of ECK Power to me on Thursday, October 22. After dinner, we left the table and walked out to our cars in the parking lot. There he shook my hand and hugged my wife. The significance of this evening was strong in all our minds.

October 9 was the day the Living ECK Master asked if I knew my spiritual name. We had initially met in a warehouse aisle to discuss privately the changing of the guard at the World Wide Seminar. This meeting took place during lunch, when most of the staff had left the building. If we had been seen together too often in the days immediately before the seminar, it would have been cause for unnecessary speculation. Hundreds of last-minute details left no time to fend off the curious. After lunch he slipped back to his office, and I dove into preparing an array of printing jobs for the press.

Later that afternoon, the Living ECK Master dropped by again. In the darkroom, he asked, "Do you know your spiritual name?"

"Yes," I said. "Z!"

"What?"

A noisy ceiling fan was on for circulation, and he did not hear me. So I repeated: "Z!" That is my true identity for all time. Paul had given it to me in the early 1970s.

"How about *Wah* Z?" he asked.

The added syllable meant the Inner Master working with initiates in a particular way on the spiritual planes. Z, or *Wah* Z, means the Secret Doctrine.

There is no way to describe my feelings during the days preceding the seminar. The ball games went on as usual as the season wound down. My playing ability had seen a remarkable improvement. At times I even looked and played as I had ten years earlier, in my best days on the ball field.

The presses were running full speed as we rushed to complete all the printing jobs before the seminar. During one of his darkroom visits, the Living ECK Master suggested I have an official photo made. The initiates would want a picture from such a momentous occasion as was about to take place. "Get five thousand," he said. Taken aback at the large quantity, I raised my eyebrows. "That should cover the people at the seminar," he added. "We can get more later."

So, in between everything else, with the clock ticking, I

walked my fingers through the Yellow Pages to find a photographer willing to fill such a large order in the week given to do it.

Finally, after several bids, I chose a photographer whose studio was twenty minutes from the ECK Office. His place was sequestered in a residential area. There was really too much work in the printing department to waste much time on taking pictures, so the appointment was set for the lunch hour. The order for five thousand black-and-white photos made the photographer both happy and cautious. How would I pay? In this case he wanted the reassuring color of green cash: But no hard feelings, friend. I arranged to get him a down payment from the office.

The photo session was to be done secretly. This posed a problem, since the appointment was during lunch hour— and I was to wear a suit. Where could I change from my printing clothes into the suit and avoid anyone who might ask embarrassing questions? ("To the dentist in a suit? Really!") Usually at work I wore a splattered printer's apron. It was washed often enough, but nothing could rid it of photographic stains. Anyone who saw me in a suit was sure to ask questions.

So I drove to a service station a block from the office. There I slipped into the washroom and put on a suit. The same station served on my return to the office, after the photo session was over.

When the proofs came back from the photographer, I was shocked at my appearance. My face was pale and drawn. The illness, and the pressures in the camera department, had melted entirely too much flesh from my face and neck.

It never was a thrill to study my face in the mirror, not even while shaving. I kept my eyes on my beard and did not look for signs of physical wear and tear. My loss of weight had caught me by surprise. In the photos I looked like a tired chicken caught in two contrasting poses: one smiling, the other stern. Both pictures were appalling.

Whoever that character was, it certainly wasn't me! The Living ECK Master finally selected the more serious of the two poses for the official photo. At least no one could say I got this job through my looks.

However, a question remained in the back of my mind: Was this whole thing a dry run, as in 1980? There was no point in worrying about it, so I just kept plugging away at whatever job the ECK had put at hand.

The prospect of facing a sea of five thousand faces at the seminar was hard on the nerves, but I knew that the ECK would provide me with whatever word or action was required.

Ray, an old friend from the service, had written a long letter to me back in mid-August. He recounted his years of doubt about ECK. The problem, he admitted, was not the ECK, but his own restless mind. Years ago I had gone for the ECK like a bee to honey, but he wanted to continue as an independent researcher, unbound by the creeds of any group.

Ray is a thoughtful individual with a penetrating mind. What bothered him most was not the ECK Itself, but some of the ECK books, which had a curious effect upon him. Rather than helping him find solutions in life, they seemed more often than not to scatter the pieces of the jigsaw puzzle even further afield. He was quick to admit that his efforts to advance spiritually had come to a halt six months ago. Despite all his reservations about ECK, he was determined to order the ECK Satsang discourses and break out of his spiritual malaise.

His decision to join ECKANKAR delighted me. It seemed to be a sign from ECK that he was the forerunner of a whole new wave of people who would make their way to these wonderful teachings of ECK.

Ray and I went back a long way together. Back in 1968, the summer before my discharge from the military, I unwittingly broke a spiritual law by typing up a copy of one of my ECK discourses for him. Paul Twitchell had not yet put into writing the dangers of sharing the secret teachings without the Mahanta's permission.

My enthusiasm for ECK was wholehearted: Everyone was to know about It, especially my friends. In my wild enthusiasm, I often forgot to respect their personal spiritual leanings. The ECK Itself does not care whether anyone makes the conscious choice to follow It to heaven. Every religious group is of the ECK; It is all life. The difference is only in the directness of the return to God.

In his letter Ray perhaps foresaw my becoming the spiritual leader of ECK in the near future. "I hope you advance quickly to the position of certified 'other plane' instructor!" he wrote. "We shall see."

A storybook ending would have Ray become a student of ECK, study the discourses, and then reach the Top of the Mountain. This was not the case. All he needed at the moment was that one year of discourse study to give him a boost in his independent search for God.

Each of us has one valuable life to lead at a time. How we use it to unravel the mysteries of life is really our own business. What is the best way to enlightenment? There are more approaches to God than birds in the fields of earth, yet the quickest way of all is ECK.

What would my mission be?

Already in November 1978, the ECK-Vidya had foretold a major change of direction for ECKANKAR during my cycle as the Mahanta, the Living ECK Master. Fubbi Quantz revealed my mission to me on the inner planes, in another dimension of time and space. There he pointed to a water channel (the ECK teachings) that needed cleaning. While scrubbing my section of the channel, I noted that the entire channel was subdivided into a number of well-defined units. Each represented the time frame of a certain Living ECK Master from the past or future.

The water channel was like a plumbing pipe with an elbow joint: The channel made a right-angle turn at the elbow joint.

Fubbi Quantz said that during my term of office the teachings of ECK would be given to people in a wholly new way. A completely new direction would occur during my time. The near future would see a historic turning point in the manner of teaching ECK.

I cleaned and scrubbed my section of the channel so that it glistened. It was a startling thing to see the well-defined turn in the presentation of ECK that lay ahead. My section of the channel was a link between two entirely different directions in ECK. And because the time frame of each Living ECK Master's span of service was so well laid out, each of them constantly urged the initiates of his time: ''Be aware of this moment. Why hurry the natural order of your spiritual progress?''

This meant that each person would get from the ECK teachings exactly what he needed during the period of history in which he came to the Living ECK Master. Any change foretold by the ECK-Vidya needed to follow its natural course, as a river might wind lazily to the sea. Everything in creation was in its rightful place at this, and every, moment.

The car trip with the family to Anaheim, California, passed with a sense of quiet expectation and promise—yet also with the conflict of knowing that our lives would never be the same.

I thought of Eisenhower, the thirty-fourth president of the United States, who served his country out of a sense of duty. Destiny had arranged for his training and education so that he might have all the qualifications at his appointed hour, to assume the leadership of his people. His was an unconscious preparation.

Paul Twitchell, however, had started to prepare me for this twenty-second day of October, eleven years ago. The thought of someday becoming the Living ECK Master often caused an overpowering reaction in me, so that I frequently awoke bewildered in the morning. It took years of buffeting by the ECK to flail from me the self-defeating traits of doubt and uncertainty.

It was in my destiny to tell people about God's love and where to find it. But there would be little enough thanks for this service; more often, ridicule and persecution. The small in spirit are quick to destroy the good and beautiful things around them. Unable to reach greatness themselves, they want to stop everyone else from attaining it.

No great deed of history was ever accomplished by a person of dull understanding. Greatness, as we know in ECK, depends upon the internal workings of the Holy Spirit; never upon mankind alone. Therefore, those who serve God, in whatever station of life, are humble. Humility is a servant of God, not of self.

I felt more than a hundred years old as we checked into the seminar hotel; a room was reserved in our name. The Rod of ECK Power had already been passed to me at midnight on Thursday, October 22. The details of ECK initiations are to remain in the golden hall of silence, and so even mine remains a blank page in history.

The outer ceremony of my having received the Rod of ECK Power was originally set for Saturday night. The Living ECK Master first drew up plans to conduct it then, after his talk, in a suite upstairs in the hotel. But on Friday night, twenty-four hours earlier than expected, his secretary called me into his suite next door. With only the Living ECK Master and me present, the completion of the ancient inner and outer ritual of the Passing of the Rod of ECK Power took place.

Afterwards I returned to my room and told my wife and our eight-year-old daughter of my new spiritual office. My daughter was afraid she had lost her father to ECK. But in a little while she settled down, and my wife and I returned to the same suite I had left a short while ago.

A group of about twenty Higher Initiates were already present in the room. They were being given the honor of hearing the news first. Electricity was in the air, which fairly crackled with energy. The group did a HU chant of several minutes, and Darwin Gross made the announcement that he had stepped aside as the Living ECK Master; I was his successor. A stillness fell upon the initiates as the meaning of his words sank in. Then they came forward with their greetings. Patti Simpson made for the door. Gross called after her, "Remember, you can only tell *one* person!"

"Fine!" she said. "I've got a friend on the Associated Press wire service." That drew quite a laugh as she hurriedly shut the door behind her.

Homer Carlile, who had been chairman of the Board of Trustees until recently, said, "Now people will laugh at any of your stories, even if they're not funny." He knew this from personal experience. A mellowness lay behind the humor in his eyes.

Someday, a few of the twenty-some people who were in the room that night will give their impressions of this momentous occasion in spiritual history. But by the time of that gathering, my inner and outer initiations had already occurred.

On stage Saturday night for my first address to the ECK chelas, I faced that sea of faces that had so been on my mind all these months. The thought of this moment had actually terrified me for years, but now was the time that my service to the SUGMAD was to begin. There are pictures of Darwin Gross introducing me to the audience, so there is little purpose in recounting my feelings at that moment. My feelings will be obvious to anyone who contemplates upon the pictures.

The ECK was flowing down into me from above. The Force was strong, like a waterfall of golden Light. It vibrated with unlimited knowingness, intelligence, good-ness, and above all, love. So this is what it felt like to hold the Rod of ECK Power!

The weeks before the seminar had gone fast, giving me little opportunity to prepare even the one talk, which had originally been set for Sunday morning. Suddenly I was on the program for Saturday night. What could I say to reach the heart of Soul? I felt small and weak in the face of the spiritual duties that lay ahead.

In the little time available to prepare for that talk, I was given ageless wisdom from the ECK though my young daughter, who sat on the hotel bed watching TV. Out of the blue she turned to me and said, ''Talk like you're talk-ing to only one person, Daddy!'' The ECK had spoken through her with the ECK-Vidya, the Golden-tongued Wisdom, and I did exactly as It said.

The Sound and Light of ECK comes down into the Mahanta, the Living ECK Master and is then dispersed outwardly to all. An initiate from Nevada saw a beautiful medium blue light cover the stage; it was like a mystical fog. This was the Blue Light of the Mahanta coming through the Rod of ECK Power. Moreover, the Sound of ECK may be felt rather than heard. A man from northern California felt the ECK Current washing upon and through him as though he were standing in the breakers down at the beach.

When the talk ended, I jumped from the edge of the stage to meet the ECK initiates. For many, this was the Darshan: the outer meeting with the Living ECK Master and being recognized by him. Many did not know it, but public hand-shaking, as the means of giving the Darshan, would soon be a thing of the past.

Anyone in the audience can receive the Darshan during the Master's talk. The crowds at the ECK seminars had grown so big over the years that it was becoming impracti-cal to continue the slow walk through the crowd to shake hands. The young, weak, and elderly were being crushed by others in the rush to meet the Living ECK Master. ECKANKAR had taken on the air of a personality group, which it was not at all.

But my object was to make the necessary changes slowly. It was enough of a trauma for many ECKists to reexamine their loyalties at this seminar. In other words, were they following the ECK or the personality of a Master?

My direction from the SUGMAD at the handshaking session was to remain in the main hall until the last person had come to shake hands. Gross had mentioned backstage to stay for only a little while, then leave. As the session passed an hour, he sent a messenger downstairs to have me come up to my room and rest. But our relationship had changed. No longer was he my Master: The SUGMAD was.

Months later it became evident that Gross had himself become attached to his former duties. The teacher of detachment had become attached. He did not want to let go the reins of his old job. This illustrates perfection as an ongoing quest, even for those high in the spiritual hierarchy.

As I continued to shake hands, a chela sat back to watch this ancient reenactment of the seeker meeting the Wayshower, the one who can show Soul the best way to the Kingdom of God. The observer saw the love bond between the chelas and the Master grow stronger as each individual greeted him. Finally, he too moved closer for the Darshan; taking a seat three feet from the handshaking. And as he continued to watch, an overwhelming feeling of love and security swept over him from the Mahanta.

For my part, I was drained. The ECK is limitless, but an individual who is a channel for It keeps nothing back for himself.

A boy, about five years old, came in the line of waiting people. He pulled down the corners of his mouth with his fingers and asked, "Why do you look like this?" His par-

211

ents were mortified. "I'm very tired," I said. "It's been a long day." He understood. And after he left, I felt surprisingly better. The freshness and honesty of his question got me through the rest of the session.

After the seminar my thoughts were already on the Pacific trip with Don Ginn and Helen Baird. After that trip, which ended right before Thanksgiving, stacks of letters from well-wishers were in the mail. But it was possible to answer only so very few of them.

Much else occurred during those historic days of the transition, but the law of silence renders them as blank pages in the history of ECK. A great change had come into my life. Now I was to learn the duties of ECK Mastership firsthand.

This time, like an exasperated parent, Yaubl Sacabi startled her with a shout, "Harold was selected by SUGMAD and the Nine Silent Ones!"

11

The Endless Journey to God

Shortly after my first visit to the God Plane in 1970, I had permission from Peddar Zaskq to assist people in their dream states via Soul Travel. Most people are unaware of the spiritual guidance from the Adepts of the Vairagi Order. Spiritual rigidity from social restraints shuts down their faculty for remembering inner travel.

But on occasion someone does recall these encounters. By way of explanation, I wore glasses for years until finally switching to contact lenses in 1982. A woman, who came into ECK in January 1973, had a dream of a young man who visited her in the hospital on the Astral Plane, where she awoke nightly to work off karma. He looked like an intern in his white jacket and dark trousers. She remembered him as slight in build, gentle in demeanor, and he wore dark-rimmed glasses. This was Z, the Soul Traveler, the spiritual side of myself.

He said to her, "Every so often we go around to places like this and tell people about ECKANKAR."

Never after that did she find herself trapped in that small, dismal hospital room working off karma. Z had already begun his work with the Vairagi Order in 1970, and now he released her from this self-made prison. The ECK Travelers know how to free an individual from such tombs of karma on the inner planes. They serve the SUGMAD as liberators of Soul, but always under the direction of the Living ECK Master of the times.

The fact that I wore glasses caused problems for other chelas who met me in the higher worlds after October 1981. When they entered the Wisdom Temple to keep an appointment with me, the Light of ECK around us was so bright that Its reflection off my glasses blinded them. One gentleman even asked me to kindly remove them, which I did. But he got stronger in Spirit over the coming months and could then handle more of the Light of God without discomfort. It was no longer necessary to remove my glasses to avoid blinding him.

At least one initiate knew that I had originally been scheduled to accept the leadership of ECKANKAR in October 1980. In June of that year, she had a dream in which she was on her way to the World Wide Seminar. Crowds of people blocked all entrances to the auditorium. Her sense of urgency to get into the hall was great, so she pushed and shoved until she got in. Then, at the front of the room, she saw Z in the role of Living ECK Master. The next day she called a friend, asking this person to remind her to recount this dream of June 4, 1980.

Time passed and the 1980 World Wide in Los Angeles became history, with no word of my appointment. This delay perplexed her, because her dream in June had been so real that she would have staked her life upon it. But it was not until October 1981 that her dream finally came true. She then learned to trust her revelations in ECK.

This miracle of revelation belongs to the children of ECK, if to no one else. An initiate wrote of her little boy who awoke one morning in September 1981 chanting, "Wah Z, Wah Z!" He went about his routine of running around the house, playing and laughing. Even though he was only eighteen months of age, he continued to sing "Wah Z" off and on for a month until the World Wide Seminar.

It just happened that his mother was backstage at the seminar before my talk. She asked my spiritual name and its meaning: Wah Z, the Secret Doctrine. It took her awhile to put two and two together, but up in her hotel room later she finally realized that her child had been singing my spiritual name a month before the seminar. Young as he was, he had known beforehand of the coming change in Mastership.

In spring 1981, about six months before the transfer of the Rod of ECK Power, a woman from California had a dream regarding this event. A candle was burning, and it was about halfway down. A message said, ''When the candle reaches the bottom and goes out, Darwin will no longer be the Living ECK Master.'' The candle had been lit on the day of the ECK Spiritual New Year—October 22, 1980. A half year later, when it had burned half away, she had the dream. But she was not able to see that in another six months, at the 1981 World Wide, the candle would have burned itself out.

Pseudoscholars pit the flickering lights of paper matches against the splendid Light of ECK. They come away with the conviction that ECK is hollow. After all, haven't they researched It with their brilliant minds and found nothing of substance in It? What never occurs to them is that they are like a person without a sense of smell who tries to establish himself as an authority on perfumes. The fact is, in the dark he could not distinguish between a cat and a skunk.

The children of ECK often surprise their own parents with astounding insights. A mother, unable to afford the flight to Anaheim and the World Wide Seminar, visited a city close to home in the Midwest. At midnight she awoke to find her three-year-old daughter sitting up in bed. ''What are you doing?'' she asked.

Her daughter replied, "Who's that man with Darji [Darwin Gross]?"

"What do you mean?"

"That man with the glasses," she answered, pointing to the foot of the bed and leaning forward.

"Is it Paul or Rebazar?" asked her mother.

"No," the girl giggled. "It's not Paul or Rebazar!"

"How do you know *that?*"

"Mom, he's got *glasses* on!"

The next Monday the pieces fell into place when a friend called to tell her there was a new Living ECK Master. Her first question was this: "Does he wear glasses? Yes? Wonderful!" Her friend wondered how she knew.

In Wisconsin, my home state, an initiate worked the night shift. About eleven p.m. his brother called to ask for help. His herd of holstein heifers had just broken out of their fence and were last seen by a neighbor, heading for parts unknown. Roughly an hour later, the two men were tracking the cattle out beyond the "back forty" and into the thickets.

They could not help but notice the unusual glow of light in the sky behind a bank of clouds. The moon and other possibilities were ruled out; the bright light radiated out from all sides of the clouds. After gazing at this strange phenomenon for a while, the ECKist assured his brother that a good scientist, physicist, or astronomer could certainly account for that light in some valid, empirical fashion.

About a month later, he learned of the new Living ECK Master. In early December he finally pieced together the whole picture. He happened to ask his foreman how many vacation days he had coming. He watched the foreman's finger trail down the attendance record to the night two months ago when he had last missed work—October 22, 1981. That was the night of the mysterious clouds. Then he knew that the Mahanta had been telling him about the Passing of the Rod of ECK Power.

All who saw or sensed this spiritual event reported a unique experience. A chela in Ireland was dismayed to find himself greatly agitated during the seminar weekend. On the following Monday, October 26, he looked at the picture of Darwin Gross on the wall and exclaimed, "You're not my Master anymore, are you Darwin?" The day before, in contemplation, he had asked for an answer to the confusion and disorientation he was experiencing that weekend. The venerable ECK Master Fubbi Quantz, abbot of the Katsupari Monastery, appeared in his inner vision and showered him with love and compassion. Before parting, Fubbi Quantz said, "Go now and be of a glad heart."

Tuesday afternoon, a friend in London related to him the weekend events in Anaheim, California. Then he understood that his inner guidance about a change in Mastership had been right all along. He just needed verification from someone who had actually been at the seminar in person. That night, in contemplation, he saw Wah Z with Peddar Zaskq and Dap Ren. Only now it was Wah Z who was clothed in the mantle of blue light.

But the transition from Dap Ren to Wah Z was more difficult for others. When Paul Twitchell translated (died) in 1971, many initiates had a hard time changing their allegiance to Darwin Gross, the new Master.

Now in 1981, a like percentage had a similar problem switching from Darwin Gross to a new Living ECK Master. This attachment to a personality is a recurring reality that confronts every new Living ECK Master. A certain proportion of people in ECK cling doggedly to the personality of a Master because they do not see the ECK behind all he does. They try to make him out to be a god, which is contrary to the ECK principle of the Living Word. The SUGMAD's top agent on earth and in every universe is the Mahanta, the Living ECK Master. But never is he to be a god to worship.

Rebazar Tarzs is an ECK Master who still lives in the physical body. Once himself the Mahanta, the Living ECK Master, he refuses to allow a personal following. He guides all seekers to the current Living ECK Master. Fubbi Quantz, another ECK Master who still resides in a human body, does not gather followers either. Both of these ECK Masters moved on to other duties in the Vairagi Order when they stepped aside as the Living ECK Master. The same is true of Yaubl Sacabi, who held no attachments to his old position as the Living ECK Master.

Darwin Gross alone, of them all, did not understand. The spiritual principle is that the SUGMAD gives sole responsibility for the leadership of ECK to the new Living ECK Master. Gross's failure to understand attachment versus the SUGMAD's will precipitated the spiritual crisis that led to his dismissal from the Vairagi Order in late 1983. It remains one of the saddest chapters in the contemporary history of ECKANKAR.

Gross was not the only one with trouble in accepting the transition. A chela from the West Coast had a dream on Friday before dawn at the World Wide Seminar in Anaheim. In it, she saw Diana Stanley's painting of "The Passing of the Rod of ECK Power." Stanley had painted it in commemoration of Darwin Gross's acceptance of the ECK leadership in 1971, following Paul Twitchell's translation (death). But in this chela's dream, Gross was no longer in his original place in the painting. Instead, he was below and to the left of his normal position. The spot he had vacated was now filled with a shaft of white Light.

When she first heard that the Rod of ECK Power had been given to me, she was greatly upset. But she explained away her distress as coming from emotional upsets in her own life, certainly not from an attachment to any Master. Although she was wrong in her estimation, it would be up to her to resolve the error.

Another person saw the spiritual changing of the guard a few days before the seminar. Wah Z came to her during contemplation, and she thought, How nice, but why is he here instead of Dap Ren? Earlier that day, as she had looked at Darwin Gross's picture, he spoke to her via the inner channels of the mind. "I'm not the Living ECK Master." Like the initiate from Ireland, she knew then that her spiritual life was now in new hands.

A final example is given here of the active spiritual power of the ECK. The initiates who truly follow the Mahanta are given straight advice from the ECK Masters of the Vairagi Order. There is no excuse for ignorance in ECK. Every opportunity is afforded the individual to align himself with the Sound Current, which flows to him directly through the Mahanta, the Living ECK Master. The enormity of this love and power of ECK is unknown to most religions. While other paths to God may be offshoots of ECK, they contain only a particle of the true love and majesty of God that is available in ECK. This is a bold statement, nevertheless it is true.

An individual from the West Indies was distraught over the change in Living ECK Masters: Her feelings were tearing her in two. On the one hand she loved Wah Z, yet a great heartache remained within her. She would later determine the cause to be attachment to the personality of the previous Master, but her confusion was to last another twelve months until it could be resolved at the 1982 World Wide Seminar in San Francisco.

At that seminar, she had just returned to her room from an evening session in which both the Living ECK Master and Gross had been on the program together. Alone in her room, she argued with herself, trying to understand her painful reaction to the transfer of the Rod of ECK Power.

This ritual of transfer is accomplished in the Valley of Shangta, near the Katsupari Monastery. It is the site of the ancient Oracle of Tirmer, where the ECK-Vidya was once exclusively given to initiates during the high initiations of

ECK. Of all the ECK Masters who attend this ritual in the Soul body, Rebazar Tarzs is the Torchbearer of ECK. The overall responsibility for the rite is in the hands of Yaubl Sacabi, the ECK Master in charge of the spiritual city of Agam Des.

While she thus sat alone, arguing with herself, an inner voice suddenly addressed her: It was that of Yaubl Sacabi. Quietly he asked, ''What is there to be confused about? Harold was chosen by the Nine Silent Ones and the Vairagi Masters to be the present Living ECK Master.'' However, she wanted to savor the play of her rebellious emotions, like a child sulking after being corrected by her father for some misdeed. So she continued to dispute and argue the point. This time, like an exasperated parent, Yaubl Sacabi startled her with a shout, ''Harold was selected by SUGMAD and the Nine Silent Ones!''

From the force of his directness, she quickly recovered her self-control. All doubts and conflicts faded in that very moment. She began to laugh, at ease with herself for the first time in months.

The events of the 1981 World Wide brought contact with old friends lost over the years. One letter came from a young man with whom I had walked the streets of a small town while we discussed the teachings of ECK ten years ago. He had taught me many valuable things about vitamins. It had been a pleasant time of friendship as we each struggled in our own fashion to learn the mysteries of ECK.

In the weeks prior to the World Wide, the enormous amount of printing had practically knocked me off my feet. It had been a real trial to stay patient and retain a sense of humor. Sometimes I wondered how well I had fared.

After the seminar, a report card came in the form of a letter from a friend in the print shop. He was the one who

222

had asked me to play on the softball team. In the letter, he said: "Relaxation and living fully in the moment go hand in hand. I learned a great deal about these by just observing you in the camera department in the weeks prior to this year's World Wide. As busy as it was, you were consistently relaxed and totally focused in the here and now."

That is not really how I had felt. It had been hard on all of us in the ECK Office before the seminar. The amusing thing about the tribute in the foregoing paragraph is that it expresses exactly the way I had always felt about him: calm and sure in every storm. Without knowing it, he had made a true appraisal of himself.

If the teachings of ECK achieve anything, may it be to show people how the Holy Spirit teaches through both Its inner and outer guidance. This lifetime is our spiritual laboratory. We lay out our spiritual chemistry kit on a table and make experiments in our lives regarding the far-reaching, but often unseen and unknown, laws of life. Experience alone lets us determine what is good for us or not.

Whoever seeks God with a pure heart shall find Him. This promise of the ancient ECK Masters is renewed today. We learn first by dreams. Then, by one of the many aspects of Soul Travel, whether it includes the fantastic out-of-the-body experience or something more subtle. After that comes our first important spiritual realization, which is from the Soul Plane. And finally, if Soul desires God badly enough, It enters God Consciousness.

The most direct, yet most fulfilling, path to the Kingdom of God is still love. It is the beginning and ending of all things. The Path of ECK, then, provides the way for us to receive the joy of God into our hearts and lives. Even so, we must *return* this holy love to all life. No matter how far we venture into the uncharted reaches of God, we find it to be the endless journey.

Rebazar Tarzs once summed up this matter of love in *Stranger by the River.* "The way of love is better than wisdom and understanding," he said, "for with love you can have all."

And that is exactly what the Travelers of the Far Country offer you.

These Masters came dressed in conservative business suits.... In spite of their duties, they still found time to appreciate the beauty and fragrance of a morning glory that grew in the garden where we met.

12

Road to Mastership

What is life but a chain of events that prods Soul loose from unconsciousness into realization? We are predestined to move from ignorance to God-Realization, but no timetable is set for the completion of the journey to God. And most of us take a long time.

What is the price of self-mastery? During the journey, life strips us of all venom, spite, abasement, shyness, greed, gluttony, and every negative trait that stands between us and SUGMAD (God). In his poem "A Bag of Tools," R.L. Sharpe sketches a typical lifetime in our spiritual unfoldment:

Isn't it strange
That princes and kings,
And clowns that caper
In sawdust rings,
And common people
Like you and me
Are builders for eternity?
Each is given a bag of tools,
A shapeless mass,
A book of rules;
And each must make—
Ere life is flown—
A stumbling block
Or a steppingstone.

227

What does the image mean, the "shapeless mass"? It is the image of our expectations. This image is shown clearly to us by Soul Travelers such as the Living ECK Master. He acts for the SUGMAD to encourage us along the road of life to Mastership. The Living ECK Master, or another of the spiritual travelers, may come in disguise to an individual in order to give him a blessing. The token he asks is easy to give, if it were not for our fear or suspicion.

A number of years ago a woman had a great desire to meet one of these ECK Masters. Through him she hoped to receive the blessing of God. These Masters are everywhere: hidden in cities, by the seashore, and in distant mountains.

At the time she was an employee in a mental hospital. One of the new patients was a young man with the clearest, most beautiful eyes. He seemed out of place among the other inmates. The patient approached her and asked, "Do you have a dime for a phone call?" She did not have a dime, but there was a quarter deep in her pocket.

"I don't have a dime," she replied, stretching the truth. The implication being that she had no change at all.

"Well, then, how about a quarter?"

His unexpected request made her stammer, "I don't have *any* change on me!"

The young man let it go at that. Soon after that he left the hospital, and she never saw him again. A haunting thought came to her. Had she refused a gift to an Adept of the Vairagi Order? She had indeed, but the Traveler expects this and will return again and again, each time testing the weakness of the human consciousness. Eventually, the individual makes the connection. Then he is able to recognize and accept the spiritual love of this great being. Once this recognition occurs, his life straightens out; for he is on the road to spiritual freedom.

A misunderstanding about Mastership is that a Master can do as he pleases, that he is his own law. It is true that he is his own law, but only in the sense that he is in harmony with all God-given laws and is thereby in accord with them. Mastery of the self means having the knowledge and wisdom to recognize the spiritual laws on all levels and uphold them.

By no means does this suggest that the ECK Masters are complacent sheep at the mercy of wolves. The Masters carry a high sense of justice from the Deity. They act in accordance with the laws of men insofar as the man-made laws do not contradict the superior laws of God. If they do, the ECK Masters take up the sword of the SUGMAD and the shield of ECK. They then act in the capacity of the Swordsmen of the SUGMAD. Nothing is more devastating in the affairs of man. The forces of ECK combine to burn to ashes any obstructions that hinder the will of the Eternal.

However, the freedom we desire is not that which comes from rebelling against laws imposed by society to oblige new developments in technology. During the early days of the automobile, an elderly gentleman in the West was outraged to learn of the city council's plan to install the city's first traffic lights. He was adamant in his refusal to let a mechanical contrivance order his right to stop or go. Pluck such as his had built the Old West. But times were changing. Regally he drove through the stoplights, ignoring the metal-and-glass contraptions that tried to regulate his movement. The possibility of an accident never dawned on him.

That is not the kind of freedom from restraint that is meant here. We are talking about the right to come and go between the physical and invisible worlds at our pleasure. That is spiritual freedom. Therein is the way to self-mastery. It is this key which we want for ourselves.

But could most individuals handle spiritual freedom if it were given to them all at once? An initiate from Georgia told about his parakeets and what he learned after suddenly trying to give them freedom. He felt sorry for them cooped up in their cage. So he opened the door of the cage and coaxed them to come out and fly freely around the house. But the birds went into a panic. They flew across the room and into a wall. No amount of soothing or encouragement ever helped them adjust to their newfound freedom.

The Mahanta, the Living ECK Master is faced with the same prospect when he sets out to help people to spiritual freedom. They want it but don't know what it involves. Then, when they taste of it, all too often it is bitter, due to their own lack of self-discipline. And they want no more of it. So the Master releases their bonds of karma gradually. This allows them to unfold at an even pace in order to retain balance in society.

They may make the argument: "I'm not a parakeet. Give me spiritual freedom and see how well I'll do with it."

There is a little bit of parakeet in most everyone. The story is told of a woman who escaped from East Germany. She opposed the iron-fisted control of the government over the people. She escaped to the West. Ironically, the freedom she found there led her to develop emotional problems: She was unable to adapt to the freedom. The authorities were finally forced to put her into an institution to protect the public.

The SUGMAD has instituted a plan whereby all may find spiritual freedom the natural way. It means finding the Mahanta, who can sever their twines of karma. The twines hold them earthbound, even as a tether line prevents a hot-air balloon from rising into the sky.

ECK is all about realization. Faith and belief are the long, roundabout way to heaven. They form the unconscious life which must someday be abandoned on the way to the Kingdom of God. Why accept a shadow of freedom? To realize a thing is to become a part of its reality.

Once a young child was out for a drive with her parents. As the car came to a stop at a traffic light, the child asked, "Is this an intersection?" Assured that it was, she mused, "I've seen a lot of them, but this is the first time I knew it!"

That was a realization. Small, as far as her parents were concerned, but all-important to the girl. Now she knew this one thing for certain; intersections had a special meaning for her from then on.

A similar appreciation for the simple things in life comes with spiritual rebirth. This is the renewal that lets us enter into the secret place of God. It is a state of consciousness fairly well lost to the orthodox churches. They have fixed their wagons to a nearly burned-out star. The teachings of ECK are today's shining star to Mastership. They can unfold in people the very secrets which the old faiths have forgotten.

If truth were given without effort on our part, it would have no value. The system of truth therefore has a built-in standard of eligibility to determine who may receive it.

The day I was old enough to take my first driver's test was an important occasion. It was a rite of passage into the world of adults. To drive meant having more freedom to come and go than ever before. But the right to drive on public roads is an earned privilege, much like the right to truth. Hard-won truth has value, and anyway, that is the only way life measures it out. Earning my driver's license was hard, too, but I came to appreciate it more than did my friends who passed the driver's test the first time with flying colors.

Failure is part and parcel of life, for without it, what would we ever learn?

It wasn't as if I did not know how to drive. I just did not know how to drive for the examiner. Ever since my brothers and I were six, we had driven tractors and trucks to do farm work. We drove wagons loaded with grain, backed the manure spreader into the barn with the tractor's throttle nearly wide open—through a regular garage-sized door. The clearance on either side of the tractor wheels was six inches, but we were backing a two-wheeled piece of machinery. It was no small feat.

We drove tractors up and down steep banks in the woods

while cutting wood in winter. Any miscalculation and the tractor would have tipped over on top of us. So I knew how to drive. But not in a city; not for a driving examiner.

The problem was that, unlike my brothers, I went to a boarding school far from home at the age of fourteen. By sixteen, said the law, I could drive—upon the successful completion of the driver's test. However, I had never driven a car on the highway or in a city.

But I had a questionable advantage no one else would hope (or want) to have: Dad would be my driving instructor. "You can drive into town," he said, the day of the driving test. As far as he was concerned, one drive with him—an expert instructor—was all that was necessary for any human being to learn the art of driving. After all, he had taught himself years ago.

Drifting snow made for poor visibility on the way to the exam. I noted with anxiety how ethereal the white dividing line on the road was in keeping apart cars that rushed toward each other at a combined speed of up to a hundred and forty miles per hour. A mighty small line. I eased the car over to the right edge of my lane to improve my chances if a driver from the other direction strayed over the white line.

"Get on the road!" my dad hollered.

Quickly I pulled back into the center of my lane. Dad was unaccustomed to riding in the passenger's seat. From that angle it now seemed to him that I was now riding directly on top of the white center divider.

"Get off the line!" So I pulled over to the right again.

"Didn't I tell you to stay off the shoulder?" he bellowed in a panic.

And so I wove an uncertain path to town. A half hour later we arrived at the department of motor vehicles. By then, during the pretest warm-up conversation with the examiner, I was laughing at all the wrong times. He scowled and waved me into the driver's seat. A block down the street, he said suddenly, "Turn left!" We were already at the intersection. But I put on the turn signal and turned left. (After the exam he said I should have turned at the following intersection, since the first corner was too close to allow for a proper turn signal: a trick. I thus failed his first test.)

Parallel parking was next. He pointed out an opening between two cars and said, "Park it there." So I did. Then he said, "Don't you know it's illegal to park by a fire hydrant?" I knew that much, but being of German ancestry I did as I was told; no questions asked. (I failed his second test.)

My nerves got worse. What dad had started, this man would finish. Next was backing. "Pull over," he ordered brusquely, sounding like a state trooper. I pulled over. "Back up," he said. This was a snap. I could usually back the tractor and manure spreader into the barn faster than any of my brothers could. When I zoomed backward down the street, inches from the curb, the examiner shouted, "Stop! Stop!"

Visibly shaken, he said, "You didn't check your outside mirror." (That went into his "fail" column.)

He seemed to have special tests for people who laughed at the wrong times. When the driving test came to a merciful end, he said, "I can't pass you like this." My heart sank. It was one thing for him to fail me, but he had no idea how Dad hated failure. Dad felt it smudged our German name.

Failing the driving test was a crippling blow to my own self-esteem. Dad had me drive home. He was beside himself with anger: A son of his had failed the driving test. A simple driving test. I slunk into the house and sat on the little bench behind the living room door, to warm myself over the furnace grating in the floor. Dad stomped into the house behind me, red with anger.

Mother said, "How did it go?"

"He didn't pass," Dad replied stonily. The humiliation was too much for him. I tried to hide behind the door to avoid the inevitable lecture, but he sat down in the rocking chair six feet from me. Then he quizzed me point by point about the test. None of my explanations about the unfairness of the driving test suited him. Very quickly I warmed up sufficiently over the furnace to go to the barn for chores and thus escaped further cross-examination.

My test was rescheduled for my next visit home from school. That time I passed. By then I had developed a high regard for the privilege of driving, because I had earned my license in all respects.

It is the same with truth. We respect it more when it comes by effort. Then we recognize its worth. For this reason the ECK Masters have us undergo tests before they show us another aspect of truth. Truth is special only to the person who recognizes it. A peculiar trait of humanity is to treat lightly that which is easily won.

So, spiritual tests are used to weed out those who don't care enough for truth. Those who earn it, cherish it. One factor which we tend to overlook about truth is that life provides enough for all. Most of us are trained from childhood to look on the austere side of things. Many of the hymns in church are uplifting, but too many paint the individual as a sinner without any rights in heaven or on earth. "Just as I am, without one plea" is one such hymn. Strongly emotional, it makes a person feel good about being worthless.

This sort of a degrading attitude causes people to generate bad karma for themselves. They feel that God loves them more if they are miserable. That simply is not true.

Life has an abundance for everyone. It will give one as much as he can responsibly accept. The key word here is "responsibly." Abundance is ours if we use it as a Coworker with God. Most people clutch what few treasures they have all to themselves. They are afraid they will suffer deprivation if they share them. Nevertheless we do not go so far as to encourage the behavior of people who refuse to shoulder their rightful obligations. We do need to use discrimination when acting as distributors for the unlimited bounty of ECK.

How limitations haunt us! Rising into the higher consciousness means ridding ourselves of limiting thoughts. Some of us even try to blame ECK for our shortages: "I thought ECKANKAR was supposed to help, not hurt, me." Such thinking is a liability on the spiritual path, for we must keep our thoughts on a high level. We know all that comes to us is of our own making, so what is the use of complaint?

This trap of limited thinking once caught me. It took my six-year-old daughter to point out what I had let befall us. Our family spent its vacation at an ECK seminar in Kansas City, Missouri. The trip had cut deeply into our savings. The moment we got home, our daughter just had to have a pair of roller skates. Every time she brought up the matter I put her off with, "We can't afford them. Our vacation made us poor!"

Within a few weeks an interesting thing happened. Short as money had been up till then, now the whole bottom fell out of the piggy bank. Things were *really* tight. There was not enough money for the monthly bills, let alone for roller skates. It was this day, as I was trying to determine where our money had flown, that my daughter studied me earnestly with her big brown eyes. "I never saw a poor man before," she said, "but *you* are poor."

That struck home. My attitude had brought the wolf to our door. From then on my tune changed to: "We're rich! We're rich!" But wishing doesn't make things right overnight. Our finances did eventually rally, but it still took awhile for my thoughts of limitation to run their course. This was a case of karma caused by wrong thinking.

By the way, my daughter got her skates.

When we come to the point in our unfoldment where we learn to trust the ECK to do for us what we cannot do alone, we are finally on the road to Mastership. Then we walk forward in life doing Its work, confident that we are enfolded within the loving arms of the Mahanta. Everything we encounter in life from this point on is to make us into the most stalwart Co-worker with God possible. We are even afforded protection from harm.

Exactly this kind of protection of the ECK was provided for me several years ago. I flew into Denver, Colorado, to attend an ECK meeting. My reservations were at a certain hotel, which provided a courtesy car from the airport. After getting my bags from the baggage area, I walked outside to flag down the courtesy car that I had called for transportation.

Fifteen minutes later the courtesy car came along the street. I picked up my bags to put them into the trunk, but the car drove right on by. I called the hotel again. The bell captain assured me that the car would return to the airport shortly to give me a lift. Hopefully I stood out in the loading area and watched the second courtesy car sweep past me. By now I was getting upset. Did this continued delay portend poorly for the ECK meeting?

After another call to the hotel, the third courtesy car pulled up an hour after my initial call. As we drove to the hotel, the driver said, "You missed all the excitement. Somebody robbed our desk clerk less than an hour ago!"

When I registered at the desk a short time later, hotel personnel were still shaken by the robbery. The ECK had spared me that experience of possible harm. If the first or second courtesy car had stopped for me, I would have been caught right in the middle of a holdup.

That was an indication that the direction of my life was turning from self-run to ECK-run. The more we trust the ECK to handle our lives, the more It will. But not according to the limited human conception of help. It paves the way for those who love and serve It. For them the Holy Spirit will arrange the smallest detail to speed them on their way.

A personal example of this occurred a number of years ago. Another initiate and I were enroute home from

Canada after conducting a leadership training that weekend. There was a two-hour layover in Chicago before a connecting flight left for California. It was there that an ECK Master, agent for the Holy Spirit, made himself known to me in the crowded terminal.

The other initiate and I had gone our separate ways during the two-hour wait. I wandered around the airport, leaving ECK brochures in appropriate places. The ECKist and I had agreed to meet at 8:30 p.m., to leave for the departure gate. A full ten minutes before that, I was startled to hear the Inner Master say, "Your companion's waiting for you." She apparently thought we had agreed to meet at an earlier time. A moment after the Inner Master had told me to return to the agreed-on meeting place, a tall businessman brushed past me in the baggage claim area.

"Hang in there," he whispered under his breath. He stopped for a long moment to look at me, then vanished into the crowd. He was an ECK Master who had often, in times past, gone with me into the inner planes. Through his whispered message, the ECK was encouraging me to continue in my striving for Mastership.

Upstairs, I found my travel companion waiting. She had understood we were to meet there at 8:15, instead of 8:30 p.m. The ECK had done two things at once: It hurried me along to an appointment, and It also gave reassurance that my hopes for ECK Mastership were still within reach.

Peddar Zaskq was another Spiritual Traveler who often took me into the Far Country. He would take me deep into God's Land and then leave, so I could have my private communion with the Lord of All. During one such trip of exploration, Peddar left me in a country of pure Light and Sound and continued on alone. In this place I discovered something important. It became evident that the fearful—the poor in spirit—would never see the glory of God.

The splendor of the SUGMAD is such that the heart of the timid would fail in terror. To someone who has still to be lifted above the human consciousness via Soul Travel,

237

such divine splendor is hard to believe. But the Spiritual Traveler knows he must prepare his disciple well if the latter is to sup of God's magnificent love and survive the experience. But once an individual has God-Realization, he finds it difficult to ever again accept mediocrity or the ambitions of the average person.

Words are insufficient to describe the wonders of the heavenly planes. But in the following experience I entered an immense world on the Etheric Plane that seemed absolutely flat because of its vast size. The blackness of its night was rent by a flash of lightning that lit up all the land as if it were the brightest day. I glanced around to find the core of this storm that produced these searing flashes of light. But this awful light of God was everywhere, bursting forth in tumbling waves of brilliance.

The Light flashed; an earthshaking roll of thunder followed. The Sound of thunder reached a howling crescendo that made me cover my ears in distress. How could I be saved from this majestic Audible Life Stream?

And with the Light and Sound of God came a mighty earthquake. It shook me to the very marrow of my being. How could any mortal withstand this face of God? The answer swept through me like a gentle white dove: Only the ECK Masters can weather such an onslaught of SUGMAD.

It is through the Spiritual Exercises of ECK that one is developed spiritually. He may then ally himself with the ancient Travelers of the Far Country. Then he, like the Adepts of the Vairagi Order, can get his spiritual food directly from the Ultimate Source.

Where do we start? In ECKANKAR, we often begin with an ECK book. For a spiritual seeker to read a book dedicated to truth is like a businessman who orders a business manual. Even a single idea gleaned from such a book may yield a priceless return.

In *The Tiger's Fang,* author Paul Twitchell (Peddar Zaskq) takes the reader along on his journey with Rebazar

Tarzs into the Far Country. "The road to God," he said, "is long and every inch of the way has to be won against resistance. No quality is needed more by the seeker than patience and single-minded perseverance with faith that remains firm through all difficulties, delays, and apparent failures."

The Spiritual Traveler never looks back to see who is following, because he knows that the impatient and meek shall forever inherit the earth—but never heaven.

Each Godman brings to earth a unique talent with which to give Soul the eternal message of ECK in the most expedient manner. We do want to become like these ECK Masters, but each in our own way. The Godman reassures Soul about spiritual realities yet unseen by mankind. If the individual will then turn to the Spiritual Exercises of ECK, he can learn for himself the actual methods of entering the Kingdom of Heaven in this lifetime.

The ECK Masters of the Vairagi Order are Co-workers with God. We must act "as if" we too are Masters. They are the archetypes for those who wish to blend their own human and divine natures into a unified whole.

In December of 1981, several members of the Vairagi Order came to support my new mission as the Mahanta, the Living ECK Master. Although each had been the Living ECK Master in his day, all of them are unknown in the current writings of ECK. Nevertheless each, in his time as the spiritual leader of ECK, was totally loyal to the SUGMAD. There is hardly a way to escape the responsibility of service to God once it has been accepted. Every one of these Masters knew this firsthand. Furthermore, none had any desire to turn away from the power of the Word, the ECK, which illuminated and transformed them. For in It they moved and had their being.

These Masters came dressed in conservative business suits. The face of each man was etched with lines of wisdom and compassion seldom found among the human race. Now each governed some region of the universe, serving under the direction of the spiritual hierarchy. Their eyes all shone with unspeakable joy, and all carried themselves with calmness and dignity. Each was in complete harmony with the Audible Life Stream (the ECK) that flowed through him as instrument of the great SUGMAD.

In spite of their duties, the ECK Masters still found time to appreciate the beauty and fragrance of a morning glory that grew in the garden where we met. One of the ECK Masters was particularly enraptured by the musical notes of birds, for in their songs he heard the haunting reverberation of HU, the ancient name of God.

I could never return to what my life had been before the Sound and Light of God entered it. The Light and Sound let me perceive the full richness of this earthly life—and also allow me to explore the infinite worlds of God on the other side of the curtain of life.

One afternoon I lay down on the living-room floor with a pillow from the couch and an old blue blanket. I created a spiritual technique in contemplation to see if it would open a vista so far unknown. Immediately I was in the Soul body, stationed on a planet in the spiritual worlds that was created perhaps just for this moment. As in the experience related earlier in this chapter, the Light of God came as lightning and the Sound as shattering thunder.

The intensity and violence of the storm grew in strength. Spears of blinding lightning ran webs across the canopy of the sky, illuminating the wind-tossed clouds. All this expressed the awesome might of God's Word, the ECK. It is what the Soul Travelers of the Far Country know as the Audible Life Stream.

Boldly I stepped from the protective cave wherein I had taken refuge. I had no desire to be trapped into a state of inaction, even by the power of God. For when Soul reaches the heights of God's love, It also earns the freedom that goes with total responsibility.

Forks of jagged lightning now fled the sky and drove

bolts of electricity into the ground all around me. Yet it was within my power to maintain the unperturbed state of consciousness that would ensure a circle of protection. The entire sky blazed with intensity from the Light of ECK. This was my world. I had earned it through the boldness of my desire for God. Nothing in it could harm me, for I *was* the Sound and Light.

God's real power and love are not in the Bible, nor in the polished doctrines of man. Truth is in the Word of God. Each of us must someday become the Sound and Light, for in them alone is found the way to God. That is the road to Mastership.

ECKANKAR Also Offers Spiritual Study Courses

People want to know the secrets of life and death. In response to this need Sri Harold Klemp, today's spiritual leader of Eckankar, and Paul Twitchell, its modern-day founder, have written special monthly discourses which reveal the Spiritual Exercises of ECK—to lead Soul in a direct way to God.

Those who wish to study Eckankar can receive these special monthly discourses which give clear, simple instructions for the spiritual exercises. The first two annual series of discourses are called *Soul Travel 1—The Illuminated Way* and *The ECK Dream Discourses.* Mailed each month, the discourses are designed to lead the individual to the Light and Sound of God.

The exercises in these discourses, when practiced twenty minutes a day, are likely to prove survival beyond death. Many have used them as a direct route to Self-Realization, where one learns his mission in life. The next stage, God Consciousness, is the joyful state wherein Soul becomes the spiritual traveler, an agent for God. The underlying principle one learns is this: Soul exists because God loves It.

Study of the ECKANKAR discourses includes:

1. Twelve monthly discourse lessons (Some titles from the series *Soul Travel 1—The Illuminated Way:* "The Law of Strength," "Love as the Doorway to Heaven," "The Universality of Soul Travel," and "The Spiritual Cities of This World." From *The ECK Dream Discourses:* "Dreams—The Bridge to Heaven" and "The Dream Master.")

2. The *Mystic World,* a quarterly newsletter with articles about Spirit and a special Wisdom Note and feature article by today's Living ECK Master, Sri Harold Klemp.

3. Special mailings to keep you informed of upcoming seminars and activities around the world, new study materials, tapes from Eckankar, and more.

How to find out more about the monthly ECKANKAR discourses

For more information on how to receive these discourses, use the coupon at the back of this book. Or during business hours, call (612) 544-0066, weekdays. Or write: **ECKANKAR, Att: ECK Study, P.O. Box 27300, Minneapolis, MN 55427 U.S.A.**

Introductory Books on ECKANKAR
The Ancient Science of Soul Travel

The Wind of Change, Sri Harold Klemp

What are the hidden spiritual reasons behind every event in your life? With stories drawn from his own lifelong training, Eckankar's spiritual leader shows you how to use the power of Spirit to discover those reasons. Follow him from the Wisconsin farm of his youth, to a military base in Japan; from a job in Texas, into the realms beyond, as he shares the secrets of Eckankar.

In My Soul I Am Free, Brad Steiger

Here is the incredible life story of Paul Twitchell — prophet, healer, Soul Traveler — whose spiritual exercises have helped thousands to contact the Light and Sound of God. Brad Steiger lets the famed ECK Master tell you in his own words about Soul Travel, healing in the Soul body, the role of dreams and sleep, and more. Includes a spiritual exercise called "The Easy Way."

ECKANKAR — The Key to Secret Worlds,
Paul Twitchell

Paul Twitchell, modern-day founder of Eckankar, gives you the basics of this ancient teaching. Includes six specific Soul Travel exercises to see the Light and hear the Sound of God, plus case histories of Soul Travel. Learn to recognize yourself as Soul — and journey into the heavens of the Far Country.

The Tiger's Fang, Paul Twitchell

Paul Twitchell's teacher, Rebazar Tarzs, takes him on a journey through vast worlds of Light and Sound, to sit at the feet of the spiritual Masters. Their conversations bring out the secret of how to draw closer to God — and awaken Soul to Its spiritual destiny. Many have used this book, with its vivid descriptions of heavenly worlds and citizens, to begin their own spiritual adventures.

For more free information about the books and teachings of Eckankar, please write: **ECKANKAR, Att: Information, P.O. Box 27300, Minneapolis, MN 55427 U.S.A.**

Or look under ECKANKAR in your local phone book for an Eckankar Center near you.

There May Be an
ECKANKAR Study Group near You

Eckankar offers a variety of local and international activities for the spiritual seeker. With over three hundred study groups worldwide, Eckankar is near you! Many cities have Eckankar Centers where you can browse through the books in a quiet, unpressured environment, talk with others who share an interest in this ancient teaching, and attend beginning discussion classes on the spiritual principles of ECK.

Around the world, Eckankar study groups offer special one-day or weekend seminars on the basic teachings of Eckankar. **Check your phone book under ECKANKAR, or write ECKANKAR, Att: Information, P.O. Box 27300, Minneapolis, MN 55427 U.S.A. for the Eckankar Center or study group nearest you.**

☐ Please send me information on the nearest Eckankar discussion or study group in my area.

☐ I would like an application form for the twelve-month Eckankar study discourses on the innermost secrets of Soul Travel and spiritual unfoldment.

Please type or print clearly   941

Name _____

Street _____ Apt. # _____

City _____ State/Prov. _____

Zip/Postal Code _____ Country _____

(Our policy: Your name and address are held in strict confidence. We do not rent or sell our mailing lists. Nor will anyone call on you. Our purpose is only to show people the ECK way home to God.)

ECKANKAR
Att: Information
P.O. Box 27300
Minneapolis, MN 55427
U.S.A.